# ALLIED ARMOR IN NORMANDY

 CASEMATE | ILLUSTRATED

C CASEMATE | ILLUSTRATED

# ALLIED ARMOR
# in NORMANDY

## YVES BUFFETAUT

# CASEMATE | ILLUSTRATED

## MILITARIA

CIS0004

Print Edition: ISBN 978-1-61200-6079
Digital Edition: ISBN 978-1-61200-6086

This book is published in cooperation with and under license from
Sophia Histoire & Collections. Originally published in French as
Militaria Hors-Serie No 52, © Histoire & Collections 2004

Typeset, design and additional material © Casemate Publishers 2018
Translation by Hannah McAdams
Design by Paul Hewitt, Battlefield Design
Color illustrations by Jean Restayn © Histoire & Collections
Infographics by Jean-Marie Mongin © Histoire & Collections
Photo retouching and separations by Remy Spezzano
Additional text by Chris Cocks
Printed and bound by Megaprint, Turkey

CASEMATE PUBLISHERS (US)
Telephone (610) 853-9131
Fax (610) 853-9146
Email: casemate@casematepublishers.com
www.casematepublishers.com

CASEMATE PUBLISHERS (UK)
Telephone (01865) 241249
Fax (01865) 794449
Email: casemate-uk@casematepublishers.co.uk
www.casematepublishers.co.uk

Title page image: An unusually idyllic view of the landings: the LCTS
have come close to shore on calm seas with no German opposition. This
photograph was not taken on the Normandy coasts on June 6, in NNW
force 6 winds, but in England, during a large-scale rehearsal.
Contents page image: British Sherman crews waiting to embark.
Shoreham and Portsmouth were the main embarkation ports for the
British, while the Americans could be found farther west, notably at
Portland, which served the 1st U.S. Infantry Division, and Torquay and
Dartmouth, which served the 4th U.S. Infantry Division. (IWM H 38986)
Contents page map: August 6, 1944, HQ Twelfth Army Group situation
map. (Library of Congress, Geography and Map Division)

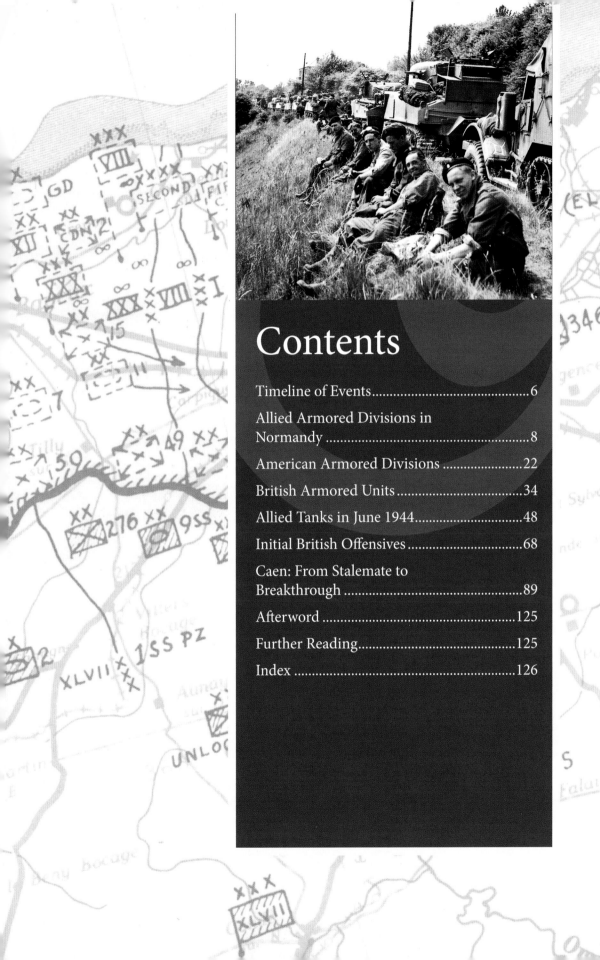

# Contents

# Timeline of Events

For more than two years, Stalin had been pressing the Western Allies to open a new front on the European mainland to relieve the pressure on the beleaguered USSR. Finally, the tide turned as the Red Army fought the German Sixth Army to destruction in a brutal campaign of attrition, at Stalingrad. Preceded by the July/August 1943 battle of Kursk, the largest tank battle in history, the British victory at El Alamein and Operation *Torch*, the American landings in North Africa, were sideshows. However Operation *Overlord*, the massive amphibious landings on the Normandy coast in the summer of 1944, changed that emphatically.

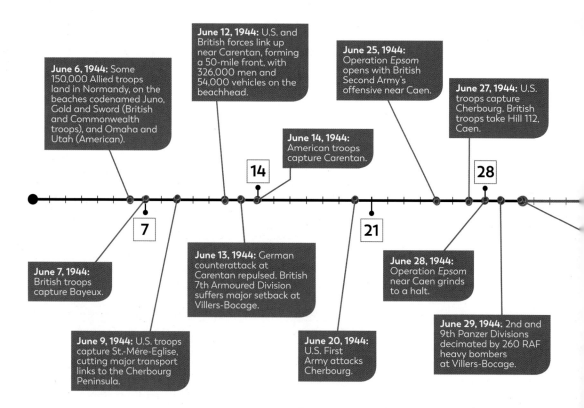

**June 12, 1944:** U.S. and British forces link up near Carentan, forming a 50-mile front, with 326,000 men and 54,000 vehicles on the beachhead.

**June 25, 1944:** Operation *Epsom* opens with British Second Army's offensive near Caen.

**June 27, 1944:** U.S. troops capture Cherbourg. British troops take Hill 112, Caen.

**June 6, 1944:** Some 150,000 Allied troops land in Normandy, on the beaches codenamed Juno, Gold and Sword (British and Commonwealth troops), and Omaha and Utah (American).

**June 14, 1944:** American troops capture Carentan.

14

28

7

21

**June 7, 1944:** British troops capture Bayeux.

**June 13, 1944:** German counterattack at Carentan repulsed. British 7th Armoured Division suffers major setback at Villers-Bocage.

**June 28, 1944:** Operation *Epsom* near Caen grinds to a halt.

**June 29, 1944:** 2nd and 9th Panzer Divisions decimated by 260 RAF heavy bombers at Villers-Bocage.

**June 9, 1944:** U.S. troops capture St.-Mére-Eglise, cutting major transport links to the Cherbourg Peninsula.

**June 20, 1944:** U.S. First Army attacks Cherbourg.

**August 12–21, 1944:** Battle of the Falaise Pocket. U.S. First and Third Armies, British Second Army and Canadian First Army annihilate German Army Group B and Seventh Army, inflicting 60,000 casualties and destroying 500 tanks and assault guns. The road to Paris is opened.

**July 20, 1944:** Caen falls. Operation *Goodwood* stalls, with over 400 tanks lost.

**July 25, 1944:** American Operation *Cobra* is launched by General Omar Bradley, to smash through German defenses in Normandy and roll out into Brittany.

**July 8, 1944:** British Second Army opens Operation *Charnwood* against Caen, with limited success.

**July 30, 1944:** British troops attack Caumont.

**14**

**28**

**21**

**7**

**June 30, 1944:** German troops recapture Hill 112 at Caen.

**July 28, 1944:** Americans troops capture Coutances as 2nd SS Panzer Division haemorrhages in the Roncey Pocket.

**August 4, 1944:** Allies capture Rennes, and prepare to close the Falaise–Argentan Pocket.

**July 18, 1944:** U.S. XIX Corps troops capture Saint-Lô. British Operation *Goodwood* against Caen is launched. Massive Allied aerial bombardment against the city.

**July 31, 1944:** British VIII Corps opens Operation *Bluecoat* that successfully drives German armor south toward Falaise–Argentan. U.S. 4th Armored Division captures Avranches and 20,000 troops.

# Allied Armored Divisions in Normandy

The Allied armies that landed in Normandy in June 1944 were coalitions of several countries that, for historical or circumstantial reasons, found themselves under the influence of one or other of the two Anglo-Saxon powers.

Thus, the Canadians who landed in France did so within divisions based entirely on the British model, which was perfectly logical for a Commonwealth country. In view of the circumstances, it was equally "normal" that the 1st Polish Armoured Division was of the British model, since it was in England that the Polish combatants sought refuge after the disastrous collapse of Poland in September 1939, and the fall of France the following June.

Final preparations before the invasion. Tank crews wonder where to store their gear. Most tanks were given nicknames, though only one—"Bachelor Boys" on the tank on left—is visible. (IWM AP 21515)

The 2nd French Armored Division was formed in North Africa from elements of Leclerc's mobile column. It was the United States that provided all its matériel, as was the case for most French divisions formed in French North Africa after 1943. As such, it is no surprise that the division was organized according to the American model.

There were thus two main types of armored divisions in the invasion force commanded by General Eisenhower. Yet neither the American nor the British army was completely homogenous in the composition of their armored units.

In the American camp, two large-scale reorganizations saw the creation of the divisions thereafter known as "heavy" in 1942; their "light" counterparts followed in 1943. Examples of heavy tanks (that came to include medium tanks) were the M4 Sherman and M26 Pershing, while the M3 Stuart and M24 Chaffee were common light examples. Of the six armored divisions that fought in Normandy, two were heavy and four were light. American tank destroyers (such as the M18 Hellcat) and self-propelled assault guns were also to play a crucial role in American armored units.

The strength of the American economy is revealed in this shot, which is not even a propaganda image. Note that armor plating added in England has been partially welded over the American markings. (IWM AP 16294)

British tank doctrine was divided into two simple tank classifications: one group of tanks would accompany the infantry, known as the "infantry" tank (originating from the First World War); and secondly, "cruiser" tanks that would exploit the gains or breakthroughs made by the infantry and their accompanying infantry tanks. Cruiser tanks were more lightly armored and therefore faster than the infantry counterpart and would more commonly be found in an armored division, whereas an infantry tank was found in a tank brigade.

In the British camp, the main component of the armored arm was not the division, but the brigade. In principle, each division comprised one armored brigade. Yet 15 armored brigades landed in Normandy, for only six divisions. Eight independent brigades also came ashore, to provide reinforcements as either infantry or armored divisions; making up the numbers was the 79th Armoured Division, with special equipment to facilitate the landings and which was unlike the other armored divisions in terms of its organization: it had an additional tank brigade that did not take part in the fighting.

These four standard types of Allied armored units—American heavy and light armored divisions, British armored brigades and divisions—will be examined in the following pages; the case of the 79th Armoured Division will be addressed separately.

# The Heavy Armored Division

In September 1939, the American army had no armored divisions whatsoever. The first two were only officially formed about a month after France surrendered—on July 15, 1940, at Fort Knox and Fort Benning respectively. Without going into the minutiae of the organizational changes over the next two years, it can be stated that the standard formula consisted of an armored brigade made up of three tank regiments (two light, one medium), an artillery regiment, an infantry regiment, and a reconnaissance battalion: in total, around 368 tanks strong.

## 2nd Armored Division
## U.S. Heavy Armored Division

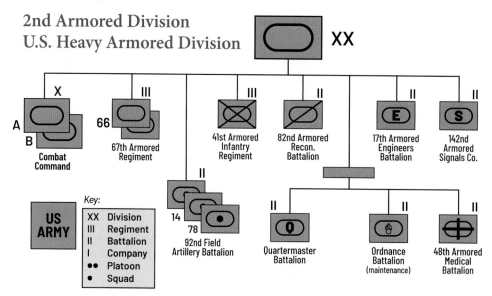

Key:
XX Division
III Regiment
II Battalion
I Company
•• Platoon
• Squad

A B Combat Command

66 67th Armored Regiment

41st Armored Infantry Regiment

82nd Armored Recon. Battalion

17th Armored Engineers Battalion

142nd Armored Signals Co.

14 78 92nd Field Artillery Battalion

Quartermaster Battalion

Ordnance Battalion (maintenance)

48th Armored Medical Battalion

US ARMY

On March 1, 1942, an initial, fundamental reorganization was implemented. The brigade disappeared; the strike force of the division was then constituted with two armored regiments, organized into two Combat Commands, namely Combat Command A (CCA) and Combat Command B (CCB). Each regiment included three armored battalions (using mostly medium tanks), with two battalions and just one light tank battalion. The organizational chart on page 10 shows the organization of this heavy division. The artillery was also reorganized, with the creation of three regiments.

# The Light Armored Division

On September 15, 1943, a reorganization transformed the composition of all American armored divisions save two: the 2nd and 3rd Armored, which retained their heavy structure.

This organization reduced the number of tanks by removing two armored regiments and replacing them with three tank battalions. In brief, the number of battalions was halved, from six to three. However, the number of tanks was not reduced proportionately, as each new battalion had four companies of tanks instead of three. Moreover, the armored battalions became uniform: in place of four battalions of medium tanks and two of light tanks, the three new battalions were identical, with three M4 Sherman companies and an M5 Stuart company. Finally, each battalion received one company of general staff and one of services. In total, the tanks numbered round 263—around a third less than a heavy division.

While the CCA and CCB were themselves not transformed, they did witness the creation of a CCR—Combat Command Reserve, also referred to as CCC—that marshalled reserves during combat deployments. Combat Commands were flexible entities, where

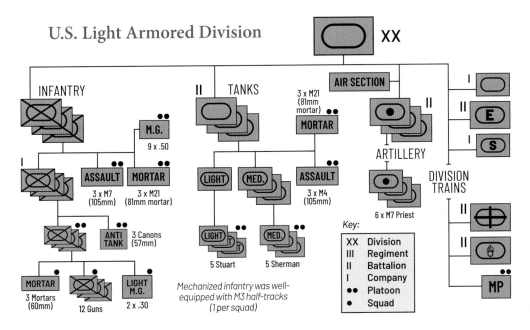

## U.S. Light Armored Division

Mechanized infantry was well-equipped with M3 half-tracks (1 per squad)

Key:
| XX | Division |
| III | Regiment |
| II | Battalion |
| I | Company |
| •• | Platoon |
| • | Squad |

tanks worked alongside artillery and the infantry they carried, to create homogenous groups able to face any situation.

In the light division, reconnaissance was no longer entrusted to a battalion, but to a cavalry reconnaissance squadron. The light armored division was 10,937 men strong, while the heavy division had a force of around 15,000. The organizational chart on page 11 shows how matériel was allocated within the diverse sub-units of a light armored division.

## The British Armored Brigade

The armored brigades always had the same composition, save for some independent brigades that did not have a motorized infantry battalion.

For the sake of simplicity, it is perhaps prudent to compare the British armored brigade with the panzer regiment. While the latter always fought within one division, the armored brigade was often independent. Its forces were more significant than those of the panzer regiment, with 190 medium tanks and 33 light ones, as opposed to 160 in the German regiment.

While the light tanks were always Stuarts, the basic tank differed from case to case: in the tank brigades it was the Churchill, while in the armored brigades it was more likely to have been the Sherman or the Cromwell.

The brigade comprised 223 tanks and 1,000 other vehicles for 3,400 men, including service and liaison units.

Each of the three armored regiments in the brigade included 61 medium tanks (or motorized infantry in the case of Churchill tanks) and 11 light tanks, with 36 officers and 630 men.

## The British Armored Division

The armored division centered around four fundamental units—the armored brigade, the infantry brigade, the reconnaissance regiment, and the four artillery regiments—complemented by various engineer, support and logistical sub-units.

The British armored division was impressively equipped, and included:

- 14,964 men, of whom 724 were officers
- 3,414 vehicles:
  - 246 medium tanks
  - 44 light tanks
  - 261 caterpillars
  - 100 armored cars
  - 2,098 trucks.

Artillery pieces and small arms included:

- 9,013 rifles and sidearms
- 6,204 submachine guns
- 1,376 light machine guns
- 22 Vickers heavy machine guns
- 160 2.3- and 4.2-inch mortars
- 302 PIAT antitank guns
- 141 antiaircraft guns
- 78 6-pound and 17-pound antitank guns
- 48 Ordnance QF 25-pounder field guns

## The Armored Reconnaissance Regiment

In a British armored division, reconnaissance was delegated to the armored reconnaissance regiment. These regiments always used Cromwell tanks, even in divisions that were otherwise equipped with only American tanks.

## The Armored Car Reconnaissance Regiment

In addition to the armored divisions and armored brigades, there was another armored unit—the armored car regiment—in the British army. The armored car regiment assigned to each armored division from September 1944 was, at the time of the landings, an army corps unit.

It was in fact a battalion, but the term "regiment" was kept for tradition's sake. The allocation was as follows:

- 67 armored vehicles
- 55 officers and 680 troopers

At the head of the battalion was a general staff with three American Staghounds.

The HQ Squadron was composed of three sections: antiaircraft defense, with five vehicles armed with 20mm cannons; liaison, with 13 Scout cars; and administration.

The four armored car squadrons all had the same composition:

- a staff with four Staghounds
- five sections of two Daimlers and two Scout cars
- a heavy section of two AEC armored cars
- a section of infantry in half-tracks.

# British Tank Regiment, 1944

Corps commander tank

OP tank (advance observation)

OP tank (advance observation)

4th tank

RHQ Car, heavy utility

Second-in-command  Liaison  Liaison

Liaison  Liaison  Liaison

Ambulance  Ambulance

Ambulance  Workshop  Workshop

Topographical officer  Ordinary  Ordinary (cistern)

Ordinary  Ordinary  Ordinary (cistern)

Transport  Transport  Quartermaster

Transport  Transport  Officers' mess

Munitions  Munitions  Officers' transmissions

Munitions  Munitions

Transport  Transport

Transport  Transport  Transport

## ADMINISTRATIVE PLATOON

There were 8 Triumph or BSA motorcycles in this administrative platoon, not shown for reasons of scale. The REME platoon (facing) also had liaison motorcyles.

> In the squadrons, the tanks would have their order numbers painted on their turrets or flanks (not shown).

## RECONNAISSANCE PLATOON

Platoon commander

2nd tank

3rd tank

4th tank

5th tank

6th tank

7th tank

8th tank

9th tank

10th tank

11th tank

## ANTIAIRCRAFT PLATOON

Platoon commander

2nd tank

3rd tank

4th tank

5th tank

6th tank

7th tank

8th tank

## LIAISON PLATOON

Platoon commander

2nd Scout car  3rd Scout car

4th Scout car  5th Scout car

6th Scout car  7th Scout car

8th Scout car  9th Scout car

## REGIMENTAL HQ
### COMMAND POST

Command post personnel

## ADMINISTRATIVE TROOP 'A' SQUADRON

Tranmissions officer | Transmissions personnel and equipment | Transmissions personnel and equipment

### ROYAL CORPS OF SIGNALS TROOP
(transmissions)

Transmissions personnel and equipment

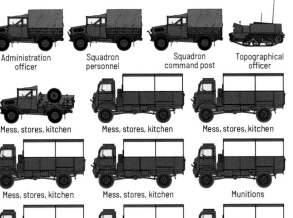

Administration officer | Squadron personnel | Squadron command post | Topographical officer

Mess, stores, kitchen | Mess, stores, kitchen | Mess, stores, kitchen

Mess, stores, kitchen | Mess, stores, kitchen | Munitions

Munitions | Munitions | Munitions

Munitions | Supplies (x2) | Supplies (x2)

Personnel and tools | Personnel and tools | Personnel and tools

Personnel and tools | Personnel and tools

Repair truck and trailer

Repair truck

### ROYAL ELECTRICAL AND MECHANICAL ENGINEERS LIGHT AID DETACHMENT
(repair and recovery workshop)

REME platoon officer

---

## SQUADRON HEADQUARTERS (SHQ) Each regiment comprises 3 squadrons, namely A, B and C.

Squadron leader tank | OP tank | OP tank | Liaison jeep | Workshop truck

---

| TROOP 1 | TROOP 2 | TROOP 3 | TROOP 4 |
|---------|---------|---------|---------|
| Platoon leader | Platoon leader | Platoon leader | Platoon leader |
| 2nd tank | 2nd tank | 2nd tank | 2nd tank |
| 3rd tank | 3rd tank | 3rd tank | 3rd tank |
| 4th tank | 4th tank | 4th tank | 4th tank |

Table based on that in J. Bouchery, *Tommy de la libération* (Histoire & Collections, 2004).

# A TYPICAL ARMORED REGIMENT, 1944

*with the exception of 79th Armoured Division*

**SIGNAL TROOP**
(Royal Corps of Signals)

- 3 15-cwt trucks
- 1 3-ton truck

**REGIMENTAL HEADQUARTERS**

- 4 Shermans
- 1 half-track
- 1 commander's car

**LIGHT AID DETACHMENT**
(REME)

- 3 x 15-cwt trucks
- 1 half-track
- 2 3-ton trucks
- 2 Scammel/ Diamond tractors

Officers: 37
Other Ranks: 655
Corps commander: Lieutenant-colonel
Squadron: Major
Platoon: Lieutenant or 2nd Lieutenant

**HQ SQUADRON** ◇

- 2 Jeeps
- 1 15-cwt truck

**A SQUADRON** △

*Tactical signs*

**B SQUADRON** ☐

**C SQUADRON** ○

**ADM. TROOP**

- 8 motorcycles
- 6 Jeeps
- 3 15-cwt trucks
- 1 15-cwt water tanker
- 3 half-track ambulances
- 2 half-track workshops
- 16 3-ton trucks

**RECON. TROOP**

- 11 Stuart tanks

**INTERCOM TROOP**

- 9 Scout cars

**AA TROOP**

- 8 antiaircraft Crusader tanks

**HEADQUARTERS**

- 1 Jeep
- 2 Shermans
- 1 repair Sherman
- 1 close support Sherman

TROOP — TROOP — TROOP — TROOP — TROOP

Sherman 75 mm | Sherman Firefly | Sherman 75 mm

**ADMINISTRATIVE TROOP**

- 3 half-tracks
- 1 15-cwt water tanker
- 1 15-cwt general service truck
- 12 3-ton trucks

**OR for example**

TROOP — TROOP — TROOP — TROOP

Sherman 75 mm | Sherman Firefly | Sherman 75 mm | Sherman 75 mm

**OR at the end of the war**

TROOP — TROOP — TROOP — TROOP

Sherman 75 mm | Sherman Firefly | Sherman Firefly | Sherman 75 mm

NOTE: At the start of the Normandy campaign, some armored regiments had squadrons of five troops of three Shermans with 75mm guns. As and when available, the Fireflies were assigned at a rate of one per troop, reduced from five to four. In 1945, the Sherman squadrons generally supported troops of two Sherman 75s and two Fireflies. At the end of August 1944, the antiaircraft troops were dissolved, and their personnel transferred to tank squadrons.

Churchill inspects the 2nd U.S. Armored Division. (IWM)

# The Infantry Brigade

The infantry brigade was composed of three infantry battalions. Each battalion had 35 officers and 786 troopers, transported in 38 Bren carriers and 55 trucks.

The infantry battalion was divided into five companies, of which four were infantry and one was support, the latter itself being divided into four:

- a mortar section, with six 75mm mortars
- a support section, with 13 Bren carriers
- an antitank section, with six 6-pound guns
- an engineering section.

Each of the four infantry companies had five officers and 122 troopers, with three PIATs. Each company had three sections of three groups, with a 60mm mortar per platoon.

The basic unit, the section (combat group), comprised ten men and a machine gun.

Cleaning weapons on a British Honey tank. It is the beginning of June 1944, the sun is shining, but the weather is about to take a turn for the worse. (IWM H 35972)

# Artillery

The artillery component of a British armored division had four regiments, of which two were field artillery, one was antitank and the last, antiaircraft.

The Field Artillery Regiment possessed three batteries of two sections, each of which had four 25-pounders—a total of 24 pieces—sometimes towed, sometimes self-propelled.

The first-line allocation for each gun was 144 high-explosive, 16 smoke and 12 antitank shells.

The Light Antiaircraft Regiment was split into three batteries of three sections armed with six 40mm Bofors cannons—54 pieces in total. The Antitank Regiment also packed a punch, with four batteries of three sections of 17-pounders, capable of piercing any German armor.

# Other Armoured Division Units

The only other combat unit was an independent company of machine gunners, armed with a dozen .303 Vickers machine guns. Non-combat units consisted of the engineers with three squadrons and a section of pontoon specialists; MT (Motor Transport) with four transport companies; medical services with two ambulance trains, a field hospital and an aid station; a military police company and various LADs (Light Aid Detachments, or mobile workshops).

At a port in the south of England, a column of American Shermans waits while others board the LSTs (Landing Ships, Tank). (IWM KY 28459)

# In Profile:
# British Tanks

A Churchill Mk VII
of the HQ Troop,
3rd Squadron, 4th
Grenadier Guards,
6th Guards Tank
Brigade, July 1944.

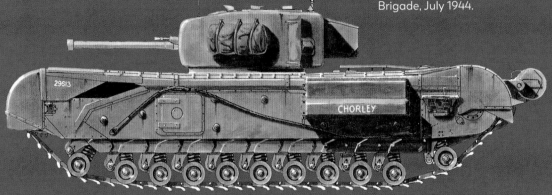

The Churchill Mk VII possessed a composite turret and was armed with
a 75mm gun. This tank belongs to 2 Troop, 1st Squadron, 4th Battalion
Armoured Coldstream Guards, 6th Guards Tank Brigade (Independent).

Insignia of the 1st Polish Armoured Division: the helmet of the Polish winged Hussar from the 17th century.

An M5 A1 Stuart of the 24th Lancers, 10th Brigade, 1st Polish Armoured Division, in August 1944 in the Falaise Pocket.

# American Armored Divisions

Of the six American armored divisions engaged in Normandy, only one had any battle experience: the 2nd Armored Division.

## 2nd Armored Division: "Hell on Wheels"

Raised on July 15, 1940 at Fort Benning, Georgia, the 2nd Armored Division was a heavy-style unit, comprising:

- 66th and 67th Armored Regiments
- 41st Armored Infantry Regiment
- 14th, 78th and 92nd Armored Field Artillery Battalions
- 195th Antiaircraft Artillery Battalion
- 702nd Tank Destroyer Battalion
- 82nd Armored Reconnaissance Battalion.

Stuarts wait to board an LST. All have been rendered watertight. (IWN NYT 26046)

(U.S. Army)

# In Profile:
# Lieutenant General George S. Patton

Born in 1885, George Smith Patton Jr first saw action in the 1916 Pancho Villa Expedition on the Mexican border, the U.S. Army's first motorized campaign, before joining the embryonic U.S. Tank Corps on the Western Front. He was shot in the leg during the Meuse-Argonne Offensive of September 1918, and spent the interwar years rising through the ranks and becoming a staunch advocate—in fact the principal proponent—of armored warfare.

On the American entry into World War II, Patton was commanding the 2nd Armored Division. He was involved in the Casablanca landings, 1942's Operation *Torch* before taking command of the U.S. II Corps. He commanded the U.S. Seventh Army during the Allied invasion of Sicily. Because of his high profile with the Germans, he commanded the phantom First United States Army Group—Operation *Fortitude*—that successfully deceived the Germans into believing the Allies would land at Pas-de-Calais. During the Normandy campaign Patton commanded the Third Army that saw action in Brittany and, particularly, the Falaise Pocket.

Regarded as the best Allied general by the Germans, Patton's decisive offensive style, combining speed and aggression, saw him turning the Germans at Bastogne during the Battle of the Bulge, and thus preventing a major German breakthrough. His career was marred by controversy—the infamous "slapping" incident in Sicily, for example—as well as his outspoken, bullish, barrack-room persona that earned him the nickname "Old Blood and Guts." He died on December 21, 1945 in Germany as a result of injuries sustained in a vehicle accident.

Shermans awaiting delivery to the field. Armor plating has been added over vulnerable spots: in front of the turret, to the gunner's post and driver's position, and over the ammunition racks on the sides. (IWM KY 12385)

The 2nd Armored Division was exceptional in the U.S. Army. One of the two oldest divisions in the army, alongside the 3rd Armored it was one of the only divisions to keep its heavy structure. Even the personality of its second commander, the heart and soul of the division, added to its gloss: from November 3, 1940 to January 18, 1943, the division was led by George S. Patton Jr.

Finally, "Hell on Wheels" was the only American armored division in Normandy that had seen combat, in the landings in North Africa. While the division did not participate *per se* in the Tunisian campaign, it nevertheless supplied men and tanks to the 1st Armored, which had been decimated at Kasserine Pass.

In July 1943, the 2nd Armored Division took part in Operation *Husky*, the invasion of Sicily, where for the first time it encountered German troops. Following this, it left for England to prepare for the invasion of France.

# 3rd Armored Division: "Spearhead"

Formed on April 15, 1941 at Camp Beauregard, Louisiana, the 3rd Armored was also a heavy division, made up of:

- 32nd and 33rd Armored Regiments

- 36th Armored Infantry Regiment

- 54th, 67th and 391st Armored Field Artillery Battalions

- 83rd Armored Reconnaissance Battalion.

At the time it left for Normandy, the 3rd Armored Division was untested in battle but would spend the following 12 months in continuous combat until it reached the heart of the Third Reich.

An M4A1 Sherman with a molded shell rolls on to Brittany. (IWM EA 32307)

# In Profile: Tank Destroyers

An M4A1 Sherman of C Company, 67th Armored Regiment, 2nd U.S. Armored Division, equipped with a 76mm gun, as yet unproved in battle in the earlier days of the campaign. Three hundred of these tanks participated in the invasion.

The Achilles was the British version of the American M10 tank destroyer. The main difference was that the Achilles was armed with a massive 17-pounder gun. This tank belongs to the 91st Anti-Tank Regiment, Royal Artillery, attached to VIII Corps general staff.

AN M10 tank destroyer (TD) of the 823rd TD Battalion supporting the 30th Infantry Division in the fighting around Saint-Jean-de-Daye, on July 11, 1944.

Before boarding the LSTs, these crews, who will form part of the first wave of the assault, are loading 75mm shells. The tubes visible in the foreground are not casings but protective sheaths for the shells. (These Shermans have been waterproofed.) (IWM KY 28461)

# 4th Armored Division

Unlike the other American armored divisions serving in Normandy, the 4th Armored Division did not have a nickname, though it was sometimes referred to as "Breakthrough." In fact, its members were proud to say that "4th Armored is name enough!"

Raised on April 15, 1941 at Camp Pine, New York, it was a light armored division, composed of the following:

- 8th, 35th and 37th Tank Battalions

- 1st, 10th and 53rd Armored Infantry Battalions

- 22nd, 66th and 94th Armored Field Artillery Battalions

- 25th Cavalry Reconnaissance Squadron.

# 5th Armored Division: "Victory"

Raised on October 1, 1941 at Fort Knox, Kentucky, the 5th Armored Division was also a light unit. It was made up of the following:

- 10th, 34th and 81st Tank Battalions
- 15th, 46th and 47th Armored Infantry Battalions
- 47th, 71st and 95th Armored Field Artillery Battalions
- 85th Cavalry Reconnaissance Squadron.

# 6th Armored Division: "Super Sixth"

The Super Sixth was formed on February 15, 1942 at Fort Knox, Kentucky. As with all the American armored divisions except for the 2nd and 3rd, this was a light unit. It was composed of the following elements:

- 15th, 66th and 69th Tank Battalions
- 9th, 44th and 50th Armored Infantry Battalions
- 69th, 128th, 212th and 231st Armored Field Artillery Battalions
- 86th Cavalry Reconnaissance Squadron.

The 6th Armored was unusual in that it had one more artillery battalion than its counterparts.

A liberation scene in a French town, near Lassay. Censors have erased the anti-hedgerow device on this Sherman Prong. (IWM EA 33686)

Final checks are carried out on Shermans destined for service. Note that extra armor plating has been welded onto the tanks in a number of place such as the glacis and turret. (IWM NYT 12387)

# The 7th Armored Division: "Lucky Seventh"

The youngest of the American armored divisions engaged in Normandy, the "Lucky Seventh" was formed on March 1, 1942 at Camp Polk, Louisiana. It comprised the following:

- 17th, 31st and 40th Tank Battalions
- 23rd, 38th and 48th Armored Infantry Battalions
- 434th, 440th and 489th Armored Field Artillery Battalions
- 87th Cavalry Reconnaissance Squadron.

# The 2nd French Armored Division

The 2nd Armored Division had auspicious beginnings back in the dark days of February 1941, when General Leclerc, commanding some disparate elements, seized the oasis of Koufra, marking the first victory of Free France over the Axis forces. When Leclerc's column reached Libya, it was reinforced, and became Free France's 2nd Light Division.

In 1943, within the framework of the reorganization of the Allied forces in Africa, the division took the name of 2nd Armored Division and was equipped by the Americans.

The constituent elements of the division were gathered at Rabat, Morocco, in the Temara forest, in 1943. West African troops were replaced with AFN (l'Afrique Française du Nord) conscripts and Frenchmen who had fled south through Spain. A little less than a quarter of the division was Moroccan or Algerian in nationality (3,604 out of 14,454 men).

General Leclerc speaks with a Sherman crew. The 2nd Armored Division's sitrep for the Normandy campaign is impressive: for a loss of 133 dead, 648 wounded, 76 tanks and armored vehicles, seven cannons, 27 half-tracks and 133 vehicles destroyed, the French inflicted significant losses on the enemy: 4,500 dead, 8,000 prisoners, 117 tanks, 79 cannons and 750 vehicles. These statistics, though official, are nevertheless to be treated with caution; while the number of prisoners is indisputable, the number of dead is less accurate as other Allied units also fought at Argentan and the Falaise Pocket. (ECPAD)

31

4th Armored Division column at the conclusion of Operation *Cobra*. (National Archives)

The organization of the 2nd Armored Division into three tactical groups and one reconnaissance group was directly inspired by the American model:

## Tactical Group Dio (GTD)

- GTD staff and command company, Chad Marching Regiment
- 1st Battalion, Chad Marching Regiment
- 12th Cuirassier Regiment
- 4th Squadron, 1st Moroccan Spahi Regiment (RMSM)
- 1st Squadron, Armored Marine Fusiliers Regiment (RBFM)
- 1st Group, 3rd Colonial Artillery Regiment (RAC)
- 2nd Company, 13th Engineer Battalion
- 2nd Medical Company
- 3rd Repairs Squadron

## Tactical Group Langlade (GTL)

- GTL staff and EHR,[*] 12th African Combat Regiment
- 2nd Battalion, Chad Marching Regiment
- 12th African Combat Regiment (RCA)
- 2nd Squadron, 1st Moroccan Spahi Regiment
- 4th Squadron, Armored Marine Fusilier Regiment
- 1st Group, 40th North African Artillery Regiment
- 1st Company, 13th Engineer Battalion
- 3rd Medical Company
- 2nd Repairs Squadron

[*]    EHR = *escadron hors rang*, lit. off-line squadron

An unidentified
Sherman during
Operation *Cobra*.
(National Archives)

## Tactical Group V (GTV)

- GTV staff and EHR, 501st Combat Tank Regiment (RCC)
- 3rd Battalion, Chad Marching Regiment (less one company)
- 501st Combat Tank Regiment
- 3rd Squadron, 1st Moroccan Spahi Regiment
- 1 platoon of 1st Armored Marine Fusiliers Regiment
- 11th Group, 64th Artillery Regiment (less one company)
- 3rd Engineer Company
- 1st Medical Company
- 1st Repairs Squadron

## Tactical Group Rémy (GTR)

- EHR, 1st Moroccan Spahi Regiment
- 1 company of 3rd Battalion, Chad Marching Regiment
- 1st Squadron, Armored Marine Fusiliers Regiment
- 32nd Company, 11th Group, 64th Artillery Regiment
- 1 section of engineers

As noted above, with three armored battalions and an infantry regiment of three battalions, the 2nd Armored Division was an American-style light armored division, equipped with medium Sherman tanks and light Stuart tanks. Artillery predominantly comprised 105mm guns, notably self-propelled M7 Priests.

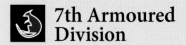

# 7th Armoured Division

Formed: February 16, 1940, in Egypt
Campaign in Northwestern Europe: June 8, 1944 to August 31, 1945

Battles: **1940:** Sidi Barrani **1941:** Bardia, Tobruk, Beda Fomm **1942:** Gazala, Alam el Halfa, El Alamein **1943:** Tunisia, Sicily, Naples, the Volturno **1944:** Bourguébus Ridge, Neder Rijn **1945:** the Rhine

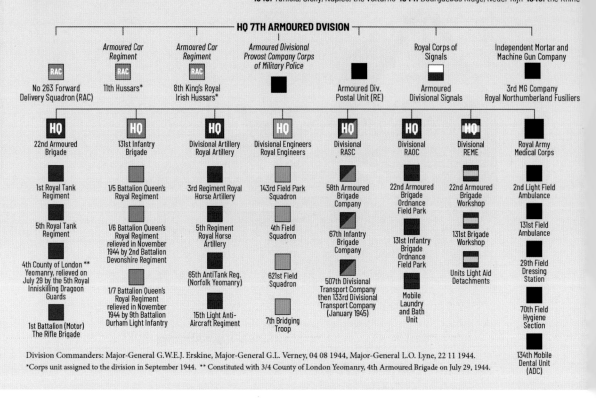

Division Commanders: Major-General G.W.E.J. Erskine, Major-General G.L. Verney, 04 08 1944, Major-General L.O. Lyne, 22 11 1944.
*Corps unit assigned to the division in September 1944. ** Constituted with 3/4 County of London Yeomanry, 4th Armoured Brigade on July 29, 1944.

# British Armored Units

## 7th Armoured Division

Probably the most famous British division, the 7th Armoured Division, the "Desert Rats," excelled during its campaigns against the Italians, and the German Afrika Korps. After engagements in Egypt, Libya and Tunisia, the division fought in Italy before heading home to England to participate in Operation *Overlord*. Its composition is shown in the organizational chart above. When the 22nd Armoured Brigade began its landings in Normandy, on June 7 at Le Hamel (Gold Beach), it had 130 Cromwells armed with 75mm guns, 32 Sherman VCs (Fireflies), 31 Stuarts and 15 Cromwell CSs.

## 11th Armoured Division

Commanded by Major-General Roberts, the 11th Armoured Division landed in Normandy June 12–18, 1944. Formed in England in March 1941, it had not previously served outside the country. Its composition is shown in the organizational chart at top page 38.

At the start of Operation *Epsom* the 29th Armoured Brigade could boast 138 Shermans (with 75mm guns), 35 Sherman VCs (Fireflies) and 30 Stuarts.

As the crews of the 13/18 Hussars prepare their tanks, a band plays a dawn serenade. The tanks are called "Charmer" and "Conquest." (IWM H 38965)

# Guards Armoured Division

The Guards Armoured Division did not land in Normandy until June 30, 1944. It was commanded by Major-General A. H. S. Adair, and its composition can be seen in the organizational chart at bottom page 38.

The 5th Guards Armoured Brigade, which received its baptism of fire during Operation *Goodwood*, used Cromwell and Sherman (Firefly) tanks.

# 79th Armoured Division

Commanded by Major-General Sir Percy C. S. Hobart, the 79th was totally different from the other armored divisions in Normandy. Engaged to facilitate the landings, it only fought during the first few days of the campaign, and resumed operations some months later, on the Rhine. Equipped with special equipment, it supported the infantry right at beginning of the landings, thanks to a panoply of specialized armored vehicles: to name but two, the Sherman Crab, that cleared mines using a flail made of heavy chains; and the Churchill AVRE, equipped with a 12-inch (300mm) gun that could fire a so-called "flying dustbin" over 80 meters to destroy obstacles, bunkers and houses.

# In Profile:
# Light Armored Vehicles

A British Daimler Mk I from the 27th Armoured Brigade, belonging to B Squadron of one of the brigade's three regiments. The vehicle, armed with a 2-pounder and a Besa machine gun was used mostly by the armored car regiments of the infantry divisions.

An American M8 armored reconnaissance car from an unidentified unit. These cars were used by the reconnaissance troops in the mechanized infantry divisions as well as by the armored reconnaissance battalions of American armored divisions. Fast and relatively well armed, these armored cars headed up larger formations.

The Universal Carrier was a multi-purpose vehicle used for reconnaissance, transport, liaison and scouting. This example, nicknamed "Bullet," belonged to one of the infantry battalions—as signified by its front camouflage and Bren gun—of one of the four British armored divisions engaged in Normandy.

37

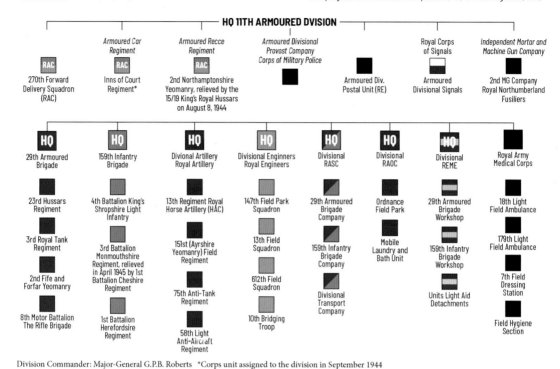

# 11th Armoured Division

**Battles: 1944:** the Odon, Bourguébus Ridge, Mont Pinçon, Neder Rijn **1945:** the Rhineland

Formed: March 9, 1941, in Great Britain
Campaign in Northwestern Europe: June 13, 1944 to August 31, 1945

## HQ 11TH ARMOURED DVISION

**Armoured Car Regiment** — RAC — Inns of Court Regiment*

**Armoured Recce Regiment** — RAC — 2nd Northamptonshire Yeomanry, relieved by the 15/19 King's Royal Hussars on August 8, 1944

**Armoured Divisional Provost Company Corps of Military Police**

Armoured Div. Postal Unit (RE)

**Royal Corps of Signals** — Armoured Divisional Signals

**Independent Mortar and Machine Gun Company** — 2nd MG Company Royal Northumberland Fusiliers

270th Forward Delivery Squadron (RAC) — RAC

| 29th Armoured Brigade | 159th Infantry Brigade | Divional Artillery Royal Artillery | Divisional Enginners Royal Engineers | Divisional RASC | Divisional RAOC | Divisional REME | Royal Army Medical Corps |
|---|---|---|---|---|---|---|---|
| 23rd Hussars Regiment | 4th Battalion King's Shropshire Light Infantry | 13th Regiment Royal Horse Artillery (HAC) | 147th Field Park Squadron | 29th Armoured Brigade Company | Ordnance Field Park | 29th Armoured Brigade Workshop | 18th Light Field Ambulance |
| 3rd Royal Tank Regiment | 3rd Battalion Monmouthshire Regiment, relieved in April 1945 by 1st Battalion Cheshire Regiment | 151st (Ayrshire Yeomanry) Field Regiment | 13th Field Squadron | 159th Infantry Brigade Company | Mobile Laundry and Bath Unit | 159th Infantry Brigade Workshop | 179th Light Field Ambulance |
| 2nd Fife and Forfar Yeomanry | 1st Battalion Herefordsire Regiment | 75th Anti-Tank Regiment | 612th Field Squadron | Divisional Transport Company | | Units Light Aid Detachments | 7th Field Dressing Station |
| 8th Motor Battalion The Rifle Brigade | | 58th Light Anti-Aircraft Regiment | 10th Bridging Troop | | | | Field Hygiene Section |

Division Commander: Major-General G.P.B. Roberts  *Corps unit assigned to the division in September 1944

---

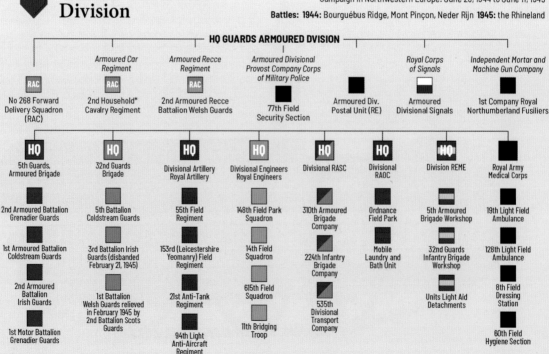

# Guards Armoured Division

Formed: June 17, 1941, in Great Britain
Campaign in Northwestern Europe: June 28, 1944 to June 11, 1945

**Battles: 1944:** Bourguébus Ridge, Mont Pinçon, Neder Rijn **1945:** the Rhineland

## HQ GUARDS ARMOURED DVISION

**Armoured Car Regiment** — RAC — 2nd Household* Cavalry Regiment

**Armoured Recce Regiment** — RAC — 2nd Armoured Recce Battalion Welsh Guards

**Armoured Divisional Provost Company Corps of Military Police** — 77th Field Security Section

Armoured Div. Postal Unit (RE)

**Royal Corps of Signals** — Armoured Divisional Signals

**Independent Mortar and Machine Gun Company** — 1st Company Royal Northumberland Fusiliers

No 268 Forward Delivery Squadron (RAC) — RAC

| 5th Guards, Armoured Brigade | 32nd Guards Brigade | Divisional Artillery Royal Artillery | Divisional Engineers Royal Engineers | Divisional RASC | Divisional RAOC | Division REME | Royal Army Medical Corps |
|---|---|---|---|---|---|---|---|
| 2nd Armoured Battalion Grenadier Guards | 5th Battalion Coldstream Guards | 55th Field Regiment | 148th Field Park Squadron | 310th Armoured Brigade Company | Ordnance Field Park | 5th Armoured Brigade Workshop | 19th Light Field Ambulance |
| 1st Armoured Battalion Coldstream Guards | 3rd Battalion Irish Guards (disbanded February 21, 1945) | 153rd (Leicestershire Yeomanry) Field Regiment | 14th Field Squadron | 224th Infantry Brigade Company | Mobile Laundry and Bath Unit | 32nd Guards Infantry Brigade Workshop | 128th Light Field Ambulance |
| 2nd Armoured Battalion Irish Guards | 1st Battalion Welsh Guards relieved in February 1945 by 2nd Battalion Scots Guards | 21st Anti-Tank Regiment | 615th Field Squadron | 535th Divisional Transport Company | | Units Light Aid Detachments | 8th Field Dressing Station |
| 1st Motor Battalion Grenadier Guards | | 94th Light Anti-Aircraft Regiment | 11th Bridging Troop | | | | 60th Field Hygiene Section |

Division Commander: Major-General A. H.S. Adair  *Corps unit assigned to the division in September 1944

38

## 79th Armoured Division
### (June 6, 1944)

**40** HQ 79TH ARMOURED DIVISION

Formed: April 1943 (First-Line Territorial Division)
Campaign in Northwestern Europe:
June 6, 1944 to August 12, 1945

| | | | |
|---|---|---|---|
| **30th Armoured Brigade Headquarters** | **1st Army Tank Brigade Headquarters** | **1st Assault Brigade Royal Engineers Headquarters** | **Royal Armoured Corps Headquarters** |
| **50** Headquarters Armoured Brigade | **121** Headquarters Army Tank Brigade | **1232** Headquarters Assault Brigade | **157** *Kangaroo* 1st Canadian Armoured Carrier Regiment |
| **51** *Sherman Flails* 22nd Dragoons | **122** *CDL\** 11th RTR | **1233** AVRE 5th Assault Regiment / **1236** 149th Assault Park Squadron | **158** *Kangaroo* 49th Armoured Carrier Regiment |
| **52** *Sherman Flails* 1st Lothians and Border Horse Yeomanry | **123** *CDL\** 42nd RTR | **1234** AVRE 6th Assault Regiment / **819** 87th Assault Dozer Squadron | **472** 264th Special Delivery Squadron 269th Forward Delivery Squadron |
| **53** *Sherman Flails* 2nd County of London Yeomanry (Westminster Dragoons) | **124** *CDL\** 49th RTR | **1235** AVRE 42nd Assault Regiment | |

Contrary to popular belief, the Sherman DD (Duplex Drive) amphibious tanks were no longer used by the 79th at the time of the landings, but they could still be found among independent brigades. The division's composition is shown in the organizational chart above.

# 4th Canadian Armoured Division

Entering the fray in August, the 4th Canadian Armoured Division played a key role in the advance on Falaise. Commanded by Major-General G. Kitching until August 21, then by Major-General H. W. Foster, it was structured according to the British model:

## 4th Armoured Brigade

- 21st Armoured Regiment (The Governor General's Foot Guards)
- 22nd Armoured Regiment (The Canadian Grenadier Guards)
- 28th Armoured Regiment (The British Columbia Regiment)
- The Lake Superior Regiment (Motorized)

This brigade was equipped with Sherman tanks.

## 10th Infantry Brigade

- The Lincoln & Welland Regiment
- The Algonquin Regiment
- The Argyll & Sutherland Highlanders of Canada (Princess Louise's)

General Montgomery inspects a unit of the 1st Polish Armoured Division in May 1944. These men would play a leading role in closing the Falaise Pocket around Mont Ormel in August of the same year. (IWM H 36646)

## Divisional Troops

- 29th Reconnaissance Regiment (The South Alberta Regiment)
- 4th Canadian Armoured Division Engineers
- 4th Canadian Armoured Division Signals
- 15th Field Artillery Regiment
- 23rd Field Artillery Regiment
- 5th Anti-Tank Regiment
- 8th Light Anti-Aircraft Regiment

# 1st Polish Armoured Division

At the center of the fighting in the Falaise Pocket, General J. Maczek's 1st Polish Armoured Division also based on the British model, comprised:

## 10th Polish Brigade

- 1st Polish Armoured Regiment
- 2nd Polish Armoured Regiment
- 24th Polish Armoured (Lancer) Regiment
- 10th Polish Motor Battalion

This unit was equipped with medium Shermans and light Stuarts.

A fine study of a Cromwell during a training exercise on the Salisbury Plains. The tank is nicknamed "Blenheim," just visible on the glacis. On the lower right is the insignia of the Guards Armoured Division; this unit was principally equipped with Cromwells, along with the usual allocation of Sherman Fireflies. (IWM H 37167)

### 3rd Polish Infantry Brigade
- 1st Polish (Podolian) Battalion
- 8th Polish Battalion
- 9th Polish Battalion

### Divisional Troops
- 10th Polish Mounted Rifle Regiment (reconnaissance)
- 1st Polish Armoured Division Engineers
- 1st Polish Armoured Division Signals
- 1st Polish Field Artillery
- 2nd Polish Field Artillery
- 1st Polish Antitank Regiment
- 1st Polish Light Antiaircraft Regiment

# Independent Brigades

No fewer than eight independent brigades served during the Normandy campaign: seven British and one Canadian. Based on the number of tanks alone, one brigade was more powerful than an entire panzer division. However, they had no infantry and no artillery. Their main goal was to reinforce the infantry divisions (and sometimes the armored divisions) and their various armored battalions could be dissociated, even though the armored brigades had primarily been trained to act as a single entity.

## 4th Armoured Brigade

**Formed:** September 1939 (Regular Army), in Egypt

**Campaign in Northwestern Europe:** June 7, 1944 to August 31, 1945

**Commanders of the 4th Armoured Brigade:**
Brigadier J.C.C. Currie, killed June 26, 1944
Brigadier R.M.P. Carver from June 27, 1944

**Armored vehicles used:** Sherman tanks

**Battles:**
1940: Sidi Barrani
1941: Bardia, Tobruk, Beda Fomm
1942: Gazala, Mersa-Matruh, El Alamein
1943: Medenine, Mareth, Enfidaville, Tunis, Sicily, Le Sangro
1944: June 25–July 2: the Odon; July 30–August 9: Mont Pincon; September 17–27: Neder Rijn
1945: February 8–March 9: Rhineland; 23 March 23–April 1: the Rhine

**121** Brigade Headquarters

**122** Royal Scots Greys

**123** 3rd County of London Yeomanry

**124** 44th Battalion Royal Tank Regiment

**125** 2nd Battalion King's Royal Rifle Corps (Motor)

With the 4 CLY constituting the 3/4 CLY from 28 July 1944 with remaining elements

## 6th Guards Tank Brigade

**Formed:** January 15, 1943, in Great Britain

**Campaign in Northwestern Europe:** July 18, 1944 to June 16, 1945

**Commanders of the 6th Guards Tank Brigade:**
Brigadier G.L. Verney
Brigadier Sir W. Bartellot-Bart, August 3, 1944, killed August 18, 1944
Brigadier W.D.C. Greenacre, August 18, 1944

**Battles:**
1944: July 30–August 9: Mont Pincon
1945: February 8–March 9: Rhineland; March 23–April 1: the Rhine

**Armored vehicles used:** Churchill tanks

**151** Brigade Headquarters

**152** 4th Tanks Battalion Grenadier Guards

**153** 4th Tanks Battalion Coldstream Guards

**154** 3rd Tanks Battalion Scots Guards

## 8th Armoured Brigade

**Formed:** August 1, 1941, in Palestine

**Campaign in Northwestern Europe:** June 6, 1944 to August 31, 1945

**Commanders of the 8th Armoured Brigade:**
Brigadier H.F.S. Cracroft
Brigadier G.E. Prior-Palmer, July 29, 1944

**Armored vehicles used:** Sherman DD tanks

**Battles:**
1942: Alam el Halfa, El Alamein
1943: Medenine, Akarit, Enfidaville, Tunis
1944: 6 June: Normandy landings; June 25–July 2: the Odon; July 30–August 9: Mont Pincon; September 17–27: Neder Rijn

**993** Brigade Headquarters

**994** 4/7th Royal Dragoons Guards

**995** 24th Lancers relieved on July 29, 1944 by the 13/18 Hussars

**996** Nottinghamshire Yeomanry (Sherwood Rangers)

**475** 12th Battalion King's Royal Rifle Corps (Motor)

## 27th Armoured Brigade

**Formed:** November 26, 1940, in Great Britain

**Campaign in Northwestern Europe:** June 6 to July 29, 1944
Officially disbanded July 30, 1944. Its elements were transferred to reinforce other brigades.

**Commanders of the 27th Armoured Brigade:**
Brigadier G.E. Prior-Palmer

**Battles:**
1944: June 6: Normandy landings; July 4–18: Caen

**Armored vehicles used:** Sherman DD tanks

**50** Brigade Headquarters

**51** 13/18th Hussars

**52** Staffordshire Yeomanry

**53** East Riding Yeomanry

N.B. The 27th Armoured was the only independent armored brigade that kept a divisional nomenclature

## 31st Army Tank Brigade

**Formed:** January 15, 1941, in Great Britain

**Campaign in Northwestern Europe:** July 19, 1944 to August 31, 1945

**Commander of the 31st Armoured Brigade:** Brigadier G.S. Knight

**Battles:** 1944: June 25-July 2: the Odon; July 4-18: Caen

**Armored vehicles used:** Churchill "Crocodile" tanks

Equipped with special vehicles, the brigade was assigned to the 79th Armoured Division in September 1944.

**990** Brigade Headquarters

**991** 7th Battalion Royal Tank Regiment

**992** 9th Battalion Royal Tank Regiment

**993** 141st RAC

Composition from September 5, 1944:

| 1st Fife and Forfar Yeomanry (*Churchill Crocodiles*) | 4th RTR (*Buffaloes*) | 7th RTR (*Churchill Crocodiles*) | 1st Canadian, 49th Armoured Personnel Carrier (*Kangaroos*) |

## 33rd Armoured Brigade

**Formed:** August 31, 1941, in Great Britain

**Campaign in Northwestern Europe:** from June 13, 1944 to August 21, 1945

**Battles:** 1944: July 4-18: Caen

**Commander of the 33rd Armoured Brigade:** Brigadier H.B. Scott

**Armored vehicles used:** Sherman tanks, then Buffalos and Kangaroos

From June 13 to August 15, 1944

**172** Brigade Headquarters

**173** 1st Northamptonshire Yeomanry

**174** 144th RAC

**175** 148th RAC

From August 16, 1944 until January 18, 1945

**151** Brigade Headquarters

**152** 1st Northamptonshire Yeomanry

**153** East Riding Yeomanry

**154** 144th RAC

## 34th Army Tank Brigade

**Formed:** December 1, 1941, in Great Britain

**Campaign in Northwestern Europe:** July 3, 1944 to August 31, 1945

**Commander of the 34th Armoured Brigade:** Brigadier W.S. Clarke

**Battles:** 1944: October 1–November 8: the Scheldt 1945: February 8–March 9: Rhineland

**Armored vehicles used:** Churchill tanks

**155** Brigade Headquarters

**156** 107th RAC

**157** 147th RAC

**158** 153rd RAC relieved by the 9th RTR on September 4, 1944

| | 1944 | | | | | | | 1945 | | | | |
|---|---|---|---|---|---|---|---|---|---|---|---|---|
| | JUN | JUL | AUG | SEP | OCT | NOV | DEC | JAN | FEB | MAR | APR | MAY |
| **4th Armoured Brigade** | 6/06 | | | | | | | | | | | o |
| **6th Guards Tank Brigade** | | 16/07 | | | | | | | | | | o |
| **8th Armoured Brigade** | 6/06 | | | | | | | | | | | o |
| **27th Armoured Brigade** | 6/06 | o Disbanded 29/07 | | | | | | | | | | |
| **31st Army Tank Brigade** | | 19/07 | o Merged with 79th Armoured Division, 4/09/44 | | | | | | | | | |
| **33rd Armoured Brigade** | 13/06 | | | | | | | o Merged with 79th Armoured Div., 18/01/44 | | | | |
| **34th Tank Brigade** | | 3/07 | | | | | | | | | | |
| **56th Infantry Brigade** | 6/06 | o Merged with 49th Infantry Division, 20/08/44 | | | | | | | | | | |
| **115th Infantry Brigade \*** | | | | | | | | | 12/02 | | | o |

\* Brigade of reinforcements assigned to the 21st Army Group. Composition: 1st Cheshire (until April 4, 1945), 4th Northamptonshire, 30th Royal Berkshire (until March 15, 1945), 5th Royal Berkshire, 3rd Monmouthshire (from April 8, 1945) Note: From February 1945, the Tank Brigades were redesignated Armoured Brigades

An impressive view of tanks of the 13/18 Hussars, 27th Armoured Brigade, leaving the shelter of a forest to make their way to their embarkation point. (IWM H 38985)

## 4th Armoured Brigade

This brigade, the first elements of which began landing on Mike Beach (Juno) during the evening of June 7, was equipped with Sherman IIs and Sherman VCs (Fireflies). By the end of the war, the brigade was equipped with Comets—the first British tanks to match the Panthers' firepower.

## 8th Armoured Brigade

Equipped with amphibious Sherman DD (Duplex Drive) tanks, from the morning of June 6 this brigade landed some elements, notably the Notts Yeomanry, who came ashore with the 50th Division between Asnelles and La Rivière (Gold Beach).

## 6th Guards Tank Brigade

This brigade was equipped entirely with Churchill infantry tanks, armed with either 75mm or 95mm guns.

A Sherman Firefly of the East Riding Yeomanry boards an LST, June 5. (IWM H 38982)

## 27th Armoured Brigade

Equipped with Shermans (including Sherman DDs of the 13/18 Hussars, who won fame on Sword Beach alongside the 3rd British Division), this brigade was disbanded in July 29, 1944, its sub-units then reinforcing other, harder-pressed, brigades.

## 31st Tank Brigade

With a reduced force, this unit of Churchills fought in both *Epsom* and *Jupiter*. Note that the 7th Royal Tank Regiment (RTR) was one of the most seasoned British armored units of 1944: it had fought in France and Belgium in 1940, then in North Africa until its capture at Tobruk in 1942.

## 34th Tank Brigade

Outfitted entirely with Churchill tanks (75mm and 95mm), this brigade fought for the first time in Normandy.

## 33rd Armoured Brigade

This brigade was equipped with Sherman IIs and Sherman VCs (Fireflies).

## 2nd Canadian Armoured Brigade

The independent Canadian brigade also used medium Sherman tanks, with the usual allocation of Fireflies.

# In Profile:
# British Shermans

A Canadian Sherman Firefly of B Company, 27th Canadian Armoured Regiment, in Buron, June 7, 1944. This tank, along with 27 others, was destroyed by Panzer IVs from the 5th and 6th companies of the 12th SS Panzer Regiment (Hitlerjugend Panzer Division). Losses in this sector were very heavy for both sides.

An M4A3 Sherman of the general staff of the 23 Hussars, 29th Armoured Brigade, 11th Armoured Division, in the Saint-Manvieu area.

A Sherman Firefly from the 24th Lancers, 1st Polish Armoured Division, in the area surrounding Arromanches, on August 2, 1944, at the moment of its landing. Note the inscription on the side: "This vehicle is filled with antifreeze 1/2 2/3 and must not be drained."

# | Allied Tanks in June 1944

When the Allied forces landed in Normandy on June 6, 1944, they had little experience of amphibious operations.

For the Americans, Operation *Torch* in North Africa, November 1942, was not overly taxing: despite bitter resistance from the Vichy troops, the tactics and measures implemented by the French were ineffectual. Certainly, the landings in Sicily, and later those in Salerno, showed the difficulties of landing on the doorstep of a determined adversary; and yet, in both cases, in southern Europe and in Africa, the Allies were acting on secondary fronts that had little in the way of coastal defenses.

The French coastline on the Channel, however, had been ready to repel attack from the sea for the past four years. True, for most of this time defenses had only been present at the ports and on the beaches around Pas-de-Calais, but with the arrival of Field Marshal Erwin Rommel, as head of Army Group B, in 1943, everything changed. The Atlantic Wall was formidable: defenses in the way of blockhouses, barbed wire and tank traps multiplied along the entire coastline, millions of mines were sown and more and more troops, of greater and greater strength, were placed in reserve in France. From early 1944, the soon-to-be Western Front became a priority for Hitler himself, who dreamed of dealing a decisive blow to the Anglo-Saxon Allies that would allow him to consolidate all his forces against the Red Army juggernaut.

A troop of British Shermans awaiting embarkation prior to D-Day. The allocated LCT numbers are chalked in below the turrets. The English equestrian smiles wryly at the crews' attentions. (IWM H 38274)

# Memories of a Disaster

The strengthening of the Atlantic Wall brought back bad memories for the British. Indeed, unlike the Americans, they had already clashed with the enemy, in 1942, at Dieppe. On August 19, three Canadian battalions had landed on the pebble beach of this small Norman town, supported by various other units on neighboring beaches. They were literally torn to pieces by a German garrison with just 28 artillery pieces. It was an unprecedented disaster, from which just 2,110 of 4,963 Canadians returned.

All the same, despite the horrific human losses, the operation was not in vain, as it highlighted weaknesses in planning and resources used.

In 1944, the British drew on the lessons they had learned at Dieppe in order to avoid a repeat performance in Operation *Overlord*: they would not directly attack a port, but would select a less protected region than the Pas-de-Calais.

The bay of the Seine lent itself naturally to the plan: it was close to the port at Cherbourg, where matériel could be landed following the establishment of a solid bridgehead, its large sandy beaches facilitating the landing of tanks and troops; coastal defenses were weaker than those at Le Havre and Dunkirk, and it was close enough to England to allow for air cover.

Shermans reverse onto LCT 610 at Shoreham. (IWM H 39000)

# In Profile:
# American Shermans and Stuarts

An M4A3 Sherman armed with a 105mm gun,
probably belonging to the 4th U.S. Armored Division.

*Right:* An M4A3 Sherman from
2nd Platoon, C Company, 8th Tank
Battalion, 4th U.S. Armored Division, in
the Avranches area. These tanks were
subsequently smeared with mud to
mask the white stars, as they were too
easily recognized by the enemy.

An M3A5 Stuart "Concrete" from C Company of an unidentified American unit. In due course, the plating covering the running gear was either lost or removed.

The other lessons of the failure at Dieppe were of a tactical nature. The loss of the 29 Churchill tanks that landed there, as well as their inability to escape the obstacle-strewn seafront, prompted the British to adapt their tanks into machines capable of clearing the enemy defenses while supporting the infantry.

Three types of specialized tank were deemed necessary:

1. A tank capable of destroying bunkers and other concrete obstacles;

2. A tank that could support infantry with its gunfire while at the same time clearing mines;

3. A tank that could arrive at the coast under its own power, at the same time as the infantry, to avoid having large tank transporters arriving at the beaches at the start of the landings (i.e. before the beaches had been cleared).

# Hobart's "Menagerie"

The War Office entrusted Major-General Percy Hobart with the task of creating these new machines within an armored division created in 1943—the 79th Armoured. This division would be responsible for the special vehicles that would facilitate the landings: to develop, experiment with and organize their tactical usage before ultimately deploying them for the invasion.

The concrete-busting vehicle requested by the British engineers was the Churchill AVRE (Armoured Vehicle, Royal Engineers). It was an excellent all-rounder—until it went behind enemy lines following the breakthrough. While the Churchill was well suited to its purpose, its robustness made it incredibly slow-moving.

To destroy bunkers and other concrete defenses, the tank's principal weapon was removed and in its place was installed a 290mm spigot mortar, the Petard, which had a maximum range of 230 meters, but an effective range of just eighty.

Each projectile contained 13kg of explosives, enough to destroy an entire house. Well-placed shots could put a bunker out of action.

Yet the Churchill AVRE had other uses beyond its original purpose. The most impressive of its "extra-curricular" tasks was installing bridges. In this configuration, the tank was equipped with a "Small Box Girder Bridge," a small folding bridge that was fixed to the front of the vehicle, allowing trenches, gullies and antitank ditches to be crossed. Other tanks carried larger and more sophisticated bridges, though these were rare.

At the other end of the spectrum, some Churchill AVREs were more simply equipped with fascines—huge bundles of wood for filling in ditches—in the purest tradition of Tank Corps operations in 1917 and 1918.

The 79th Armoured Division also employed another iteration of the Churchill: a flame-throwing tank known as the "Crocodile," though the first of these did not make an appearance until July 1944, and were not used in combat until the attack on Le Havre in September.

(Lt Tanner, War Office /
IWM H 20697)

# In Profile:
# Major-General Percy Hobart

"Hobo", or Major-General Sir Percy Cleghorn Stanley Hobart KBE, CB, DSO, MC, was born in 1885 in India, destined to become Britain's foremost military engineer of all time. He graduated from the Royal Military Academy, Woolwich, in 1904 before being commissioned into the Royal Engineers. During World War I he saw action on the Western Front—the battles of Neuve Chappelle, Artois and Loos—before being sent to Mesopotamia where he was involved in the siege of Kut and the battle of Megiddo. During the interwar years, a firm disciple of armored warfare, he was promoted to brigadier in 1934 in charge of the Royal Tank Corps, the UK's first armored brigade. At the time his doctrinal writings were closely followed by both Liddell Hart and Heinz Guderian.

On the outbreak of World War II, Hobart found himself in Egypt in charge of Mobile Force Egypt, the forerunner to the 7th Armoured Division, the "Desert Rats." Due to his unconventional, seemingly outrageous, views on armored warfare, he was sidelined by General Wavell into retirement. He joined his local Home Guard as a lance-corporal before Churchill, at Liddell Hart's behest, had him back in the army training the 11th Armoured Division, followed by the 79th Armoured Division. This time "Hobo" was saved from his hostile detractors by General Sir Alan Brooke who saw the value of the many and varied tank design modifications—"Hobart's funnies," including the Sherman amphibious DD—that helped the Allies get ashore on D-Day. By the end of the war, the 79th's inventory amounted to some 7,000 vehicles. Hobart retired (again) in 1946 and died in 1957.

An array of tanks aboard LCT 212. The crew of the Sherman in the foreground appear unconvinced by the glacis armor and have covered the driver's post with tracking and spare wheels. These tanks belong to the 13/18 Hussars. (IWM H 39001)

As for the mine-clearing tanks, testing began early in the war, but the first examples—like the Matilda Baron—were not entirely satisfactory. This was mostly because of the sheer amount of space required by the motor controlling the flail chains: the turret basically had to be removed to fit it on.

Considerable progress was made with the Sherman "Crab." This new creation did not need the additional motor for the flail, so it could keep its turret and weaponry intact, allowing it to support infantry and other armor.

Its tactical use was simple enough: when it arrived at a minefield or a suspicious-looking patch of ground, the Crab engaged its chain flail and advanced in a straight line at 2.5kph. It could thus clear a path around 2.7m wide. Its situation was nevertheless uncomfortable during such times. First of all, it was rare that all the mines were detonated by the flail, so the tank itself was often put out of action by the mines it had missed. Next, its slowness made it a choice target, exacerbated by the fact that it was unable to shoot while demining. Moreover, the Crabs worked in teams, each active mine-clearer being supported by the others. Finally, repeated explosions rapidly worked through the flail chains.

The third tank in Hobart's "Menagerie"—and the only one adopted by the Americans—was the amphibious Duplex Drive. The invention of the "DD" is attributed to an engineer named Nicholas Straussier, a Hungarian immigrant, who worked according to one core principle: any object can float if it has sufficient displacement.

Prototypes of light Tetrarch tanks fitted with canvas hulls proved satisfactory, so mass production on the "Valentine" began. The Valentine's system consisted of a canvas curtain

This LCT, transporting an M10 tank destroyer, is also carrying a number of canvases and fascines that will facilitate landing on the beaches and infamous blue mud. (IWM H 38996)

that surrounded the tank, forming a shell that could be removed on landfall. It was powered by propellers coupled to the engine—the Duplex Drive that the tank ultimately adopted as a moniker for the tanks used on June 6, 1944. The most interesting aspect of this invention was that it only minimally modified the original tank: it even weighed about the same. In addition, once the canvas was folded up and stowed, the tank appeared almost completely unchanged, and could still use its entire arsenal.

Its nautical qualities were more or less satisfactory: as long as the sea was fairly calm, the DD could navigate with reasonable accuracy. Erring on the side of caution, the lifejacket-clad crew stood on top of the tank (excepting, for obvious reasons, the driver); a bilge pump, carried in case of leaks or excessive surf, completed the outfit.

# June 6: The Menagerie in Action

The prevailing meteorological conditions at dawn on June 6 were far from ideal: strong winds and rough seas. The results of using the Sherman DD amphibious tanks varied greatly from beach to beach. The archives of the 79th Armoured Division provide a complete report of the Duplex Drive operations, from which the following facts have been drawn.

The Americans had three battalions of DD tanks—the 70th, the 741st and the 743rd Tank Battalions—which trained alongside the 79th Armoured in the Solent.

The 70th Tank Battalion landed at Utah Beach, supporting the 4th U.S. Infantry Division of the VII Corps. Twenty-eight DDs were launched into reasonably calm waters

A Sherman BARV (Beach Armoured Recovery Vehicle) drives along a column of Shermans waiting to board. This recovery vehicle was used by the Royal Electrical and Mechanical Engineers. (IWM H 38987)

five kilometers from the shore. Just one sank during the "swim." The remaining 27 arrived at the same time as the infantry, and proved invaluable in clearing the beach.

The 741st and the 743rd Tank Battalions were supporting the 1st U.S. Infantry, V Corps at Omaha Beach. The sea was particularly rough here, as the area around Colleville-sur-Mer was not protected by the Cotentin Peninsula as other beaches were. Indeed, conditions were so bad that the 743rd did not launch any of its tanks, preferring to land them after the LCTs.

The commander of the 741st decided to launch his 29 Sherman DDs an ambitious six kilometers out. The tanks were pushed out into surging waves and squalls. The force of the waves bent the poles supporting the canvas shells, and, one by one, the DDs sank. Only five reached Omaha Beach; 24 had disappeared completely. Yet solid ground did not offer the surviving crews salvation—far from it: one tanks took a direct hit from an 88mm as it emerged from the water.

The sea was equally tempestuous in the British sector at Gold Beach. The Nottinghamshire Yeomanry's tanks stayed on their LCT, waiting to land directly onto the beach as soon as it was possible to do so. At Juno Beach, it was not much better; the 10th Canadian Armoured Regiment's DDs did not risk the elements, but those of the 6th Canadian Armoured Regiment launched at the closest possible range, without endangering the LCT, of 2,000 meters. The waves were so violent that half of the 38 tanks were lost before they reached the beach. The 19 survivors, however, arrived as planned at the same time as the infantry, to support them in the ensuing action.

At Sword Beach, the sea was somewhat calmer, and the 13/18 Hussars were able to launch their DDs in support of the 3rd British Infantry Division. Though the amphibious tanks left the carrier before everyone else—at 5,000 meters out—they were hampered by the weather and soon overtaken by the barges carrying the infantry and specialized tanks of the Royal Engineers. In the confusion, one of the Duplex Drives was hit and sunk by an LCT. Nevertheless, of the 34 tanks that launched, 33 emerged onto the beach, ten minutes after the infantry, Flails and AVREs.

To fully understand the difficulties encountered by the DD tank crews, one must imagine the long journey they had to make between the LCT and the shore. A journey of five kilometers in the middle of a crowd of other tanks, in rough seas that twisted and distorted the very material that was keeping the crews alive—the poles supporting the canvas skirt. Men were forced to support these poles by hand. If they failed or if the poles broke, the sea would rush in and the tank would most probably sink, despite the pumps on board.

Yet there was one small consolation: the DDs, whose superstructures were not visible above the water level, did not therefore offer up clear target to the German gunners. They could not be spotted among the multitude of boats, and as a result none was sunk at sea by German fire.

In total, 80 of the 130 Duplex Drives launched reached the shore.

## Tanks on the Beach

The archives of the 79th Armoured Division contain a report from General Hobart, written on June 19, 1944 after his visit to the commanders of nearby units during the landings (Second Army, I and XXX Corps, and U.S. V Corps). It is a first-hand account of the battle, drafted shortly after the fact.

First of all, Hobart congratulated Specialized Assault Troops saying that on some beaches, it is doubtful that the assault would have succeeded without the mass of tanks that landed with the first wave. German defenses on the beach were solid and held by a large number of effective soldiers; the light losses of the first wave (in the British sector) were thanks, according to Hobart, to the element of surprise, to the good organization of the invasion, to the preliminary bombing and, finally, "of the novel mechanical contrivances which we employed, and the staggering moral and material effect of the mass of armor landed in the leading waves of the assault."

In effect, the infantry, which was not always led or accompanied by DD tanks for reasons outlined above, was always supported by Churchill AVREs and Sherman Crabs. When DDs did not reach the beaches, the Crabs proved invaluable. Thanks to their 75mm guns, they took out German blockhouses and machine-gun nests. The landing of dozens of tanks at the same time also limited losses as the German guns were quickly destroyed.

# In Profile:
# American Stuarts

An M5A1 light tank from an unidentified American unit. The large 16 appears to have been added at the last minute, prior to boarding the LCT. British crews, like their American counterparts, did not hesitate to cover turrets and glacises with tank tracks and spare sprockets to add thickness to the often-flimsy armor on these small reconnaissance tanks.

An M5A1 light tank from an unidentified American armored unit. Launched onto the Normandy roads, "Jumbo's" crew have stretched an orange canvas over the back of their tank for aerial identification.

An M5A1 light tank of the 3rd Armored Division. This tank is shown here as it did just after its arrival in Normandy: its crew have removed the mudguards and kept the lower section of the engine sump.

The British were proud to have designed all the "funnies" in Hobart's "Menagerie," which they alone used during the Normandy landings (with the exception, of course, of the DDs used by the Americans). But the American engineers were not idle during the preparation period; as the presence of these two vehicles show. Both are amphibious: the DUKW on a GMC truck chassis is on the left, and the GPA amphibious Jeep is on the right. They are being used here by the British—the American white star acted as an identification mark for all Allied vehicles. (IWM H 38993)

As soon as they arrived on the beaches, the Flails of the 22nd Dragoons and Westminster Dragoons were put to work. Clearing mines was a painfully slow task, as the crews were constantly being forced to stop: the beaches were crammed with men and matériel, and the infantry often interrupted the process to make use of the tanks' 75mm guns to subdue enemy resistance. But, on the whole, the schedule was respected: at H+10mn and H+7h, the Flails raked the beaches, and in the early afternoon, they advanced inland. By nightfall, losses had risen to 50 percent, but in the following days the repair workshops were able to get around half of the immobilized tanks back into action.

Having reached the shore at the same time as the Crabs, the Churchill AVREs opened breaches in the concrete defenses, though attacking the bunkers brought relatively high losses. The low range of their Petard mortars made them easy prey for the German antitank guns. Without artillery support and without a smokescreen, the AVREs would have stood little chance, but fortunately cooperation between the Churchills and the Crabs was strong: the latter would fire their 75mm projectiles into the blockhouses while the AVREs advanced and opened fire with their Petards.

At Le Hamel, German resistance centered around the sanatorium that had literally been transformed into a fortress. In the late morning, a Churchill AVRE approached and fired two Dustbins that ravaged the building. The entire garrison surrendered within minutes.

At the other end of Gold Beach, at La Rivière, three AVREs were charged with clearing the beach, which they proceeded to do under continuous fire from German soldiers hidden behind a concrete wall running parallel to the beach. Two Churchills managed to traverse the wall, landing heavily after a 1.2m drop on the other side. The Germans immediately surrendered.

At Ouistreham, on Sword Beach, a single AVRE managed to save the locks by surprising a group of Germans who were preparing to blow them up. Everywhere, the tanks were proving vital, but their losses were severe: by the evening of June 6, 40 percent of the officers of the 5th Regiment, Armoured Royal Engineers had been killed or wounded. Tank commanders were frequently hit by small-arms fire, by dint of the fact that they commanded from the turret. For the rest of the crews, losses were lighter: for example, the 22nd Dragoons, equipped with Sherman Crabs, suffered only four officers killed and four troopers wounded on D-Day.

## The American Beaches

Historians are still trying to ascertain whether the lack of specialized tanks was responsible for the heavy losses on Omaha Beach. What can be said is that the first waves of infantry were only supported by four Sherman DDs, an insufficient number in anyone's view. In fact, it seems that, specialized tanks or no, it was the absence of any Shermans on the beach at the beginning of the assault that exacerbated the casualty rates. The American tanks arrived much later than the infantry, significant losses had already been incurred, and the element of surprise had long since passed. When interviewed by Hobart, General Leonard T. Gerow recalled losing 79 tanks on Omaha and it is highly probable that had these tanks had arrived much earlier, the German defenses would have been overwhelmed at the outset.

These Royal Engineers are using two armored bulldozers to create roads and access routes to the landing beaches. (IWM H 383095)

An East Riding Sherman climbs the ramp into LST 381 in a large cloud of smoke. The tank has been made watertight, so the gases are escaping via a large chimney attached to the rear of the vehicle. (IWM H 38978)

# Consolidation

In the days after D-Day, the Allies consolidated their bridgehead and landed several armored units, while the infantry, supported by antitank regiments, prepared for the inevitable German counterattack … that never came. The British took the opportunity to consolidate. The landing and regrouping of the armored units was almost languid; an example of this is revealed in the Royal Scots Greys war diary that recalls Major D. N. Stewart, MC, landing at 2200 hours on Mike Beach, with the tanks of A Squadron and Captain R. L. E. Milburn, with two tanks from B Squadron. They then went to the transit zone at Courseulles-sur-Mer, where they were shelled from time to time.

That evening, the battalion's forces were 12 Sherman IIs, two Sherman VC Fireflies and a Stuart. The table shows the strength for the following days:

|  | Sherman II | Sherman VC | Stuart | Armored cars |
|---|---|---|---|---|
| June 8 | 14 | 4 | 1 | 0 |
| June 9 | 30 | 4 | 1 | 0 |
| June 10 | 49 | 11 | 10 | 9 |

However, in some cases, when the units had to engage quickly, the landings were much faster: the 22nd Armoured Brigade is a good example. It arrived off the coast of Le Hamel on June 7 at half past midnight.

At 0800 hours, the first elements landed, and the toing and froing continued throughout the day. By evening, the brigade was complete, with 130 Cromwells (75mm), 32 Sherman

(George Peck Collection)

# In Profile:
# General Dwight D. Eisenhower

Of German–Dutch heritage, "Ike" was born in 1890 in Texas, but grew up in Abilene, Kansas. Without funding for college, Eisenhower managed to get into West Point, graduating middle of the class in 1915. In spite of numerous requests, he was denied postings to the Western Front in World War I, serving out the war with 65th Engineers and the new tank corps. However, his organizational and administrative skills had been noticed. Between the wars, he worked with a succession of generals—Fox Connor, John Pershing, George Marshall and Douglas MacArthur—and accompanied McArthur, against whom he developed a lifelong antipathy, to the Philippines from 1935 to December 1939.

The Japanese attack on Pearl Harbor found Eisenhower as a brigadier general, but without prospects because of his lack of active command. He served on the General Staff in Washington before being appointed, in June 1942, Commanding General European Theater of Operations in London. Five months later he was appointed Supreme Commander of Operation *Torch*, the North African campaign that he directed from Gibraltar. He then oversaw the invasions of Sicily and the Italian mainland.

In December 1943, President Roosevelt appointed Eisenhower as Supreme Allied Commander of the Allied Expeditionary Force (SHAEF) charged with overseeing the Allied invasion of France, the liberation of Western Europe and the invasion of Germany. It was here that his experience in North Africa and the Mediterranean came to the fore, and, coupled with his sublime planning and diplomacy skills, he was able to steer the Allies to victory. He became the 34th President of the United Sates in 1953. He died in 1969.

# In Profile:
# Allied Tanks

This M10 "Wolverine" tank destroyer is about to board
an LST. It has not as yet been loaded up with the
equipment and impedimenta of its campaign crew,
but it has received some of its landing codes.

*Right:* This M4A3 Sherman belongs to an unidentified American
tank battalion. An additional armor plate has been added at
some point during the campaign, obscuring its white star. It
is likely that the lateral mudguards will soon disappear, lost or
simply abandoned by the side of a road.

An M4A1 Duplex Drive from one of three American armored battalions (70th Tank Battalion at Utah Beach, 741st and 743rd Tank Battalions at Omaha Beach) on June 6, 1944. The floatation skirt has been folded down, indicating that the tank has either already arrived on the beach, or has yet to be launched from its LST.

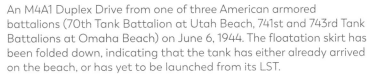

An amphibious column prepares for embarkation, alongside some DUKWs and waterproofed Shermans. (IWM H 38992)

Fireflies, 31 Stuarts and 15 specialized Cromwells (antiaircraft, etc.). It is interesting to note that during this day of intensive work, some of the tanks actually fell into the water: two Stuarts, two Cromwells, two Fireflies and two antiaircraft tanks. They were, fortunately, quickly recovered.

From June 8, the brigade began fighting, near Sully. The speed of their deployment was exceptional, as, for example, it took six days for the 29th Armoured Brigade to complete its landings—from June 12 to 18—though their forces were comparable to those of the 22nd.

Among the armored brigades that fought at the front during the early days of the invasion, one of the worst hit was the 2nd Canadian Armoured Brigade, whose 27th Armoured Regiment (Sherbrooke Fusiliers) was surprised by the 2nd Panzer Regiment, 12th SS Panzer Division (Hitlerjugend) near the hamlet of Franqueville. In the difficult battle that ensued, the Canadians lost 28 Shermans, against six Panzer IVs.

The 22nd Armoured Brigade, which belonged to the 7th Armoured "Desert Rats" Division, was assigned to help the infantry reinforce the bridgehead by clearing the last clusters of resistance. This task was by no means an easy one: A Squadron of the 5th Royal Tank Regiment (RTR) was engaged alongside the South Wales Borderers against the village of Sully. After a promising start, the infantry was stopped by intense machine-gun fire, followed soon after by an artillery and mortar bombardment. The men retreated to their starting line, as did the tanks, which were soon attacked by two self-propelled German machine guns. A Firefly was soon destroyed and the crew of an observation Cromwell, to escape enemy fire, toppled their tank—with them inside it—into a river, killing the tank commander.

B Squadron, alongside the Devons, had more success during its attack on Buffay and Le Manoir. These two villages were taken without shots fired, opening the road to Port-en-Bessin that was captured the same evening and which was where the Americans and the British linked up.

(www.maxwell.af.mil)

## In Profile:
# General Bernard Montgomery

"Monty" was born in 1897 in Surrey, but spent eight years of his austere childhood in Tasmania, where his father was bishop. In 1908 he graduated from the Royal Military College, Sandhurst. He served with the Royal Warwickshire Regiment on the Western Front, seeing action at First Ypres (where he was shot through the right lung), Arras and Passchendaele.

During the interwar years he steadily rose through the ranks. However, in 1937, tragedy struck: his wife Betty died from septicaemia. (Betty was Percy Hobart's sister.) In 1938, a devastated Monty took command of the 8th Infantry Division in Palestine. On the outbreak of war, he assumed command of the BEF's 3rd Division, organizing its successful withdrawal to the Dunkirk perimeter with negligible casualties.

In August 1942, he took command of the Eighth Army in the Western Desert and frenetically set about strengthening the British forces. By the time the offensive began on October 23, he had 231,000 men under arms. El Alamein was a comprehensive defeat for Rommel's Afrika Korps, but Montgomery's pursuit of his enemy across Libya and Tunisia was turgid. He led the Eighth Army in its invasions of Sicily and the Italian mainland.

He was appointed overall commander of Allied ground forces during Operation *Overlord*, then commanded the 21st Army Group in North West Europe. Operation *Market Garden*, the Allied disaster at Arnhem, came under his remit. On May 4, 1945 he took the German surrender at Lüneburg Heath in northern Germany. He retired in 1958 as Field Marshal Bernard Law Montgomery, 1st Viscount Montgomery of Alamein, KG, GCB, DSO, PC, DL and died in 1976.

# | Initial British Offensives

While the Normandy bridgehead was still being reinforced, in an effort to capture ground inland of the bridgehead to prevent German counterattack, Montgomery pushed forward in an attempt to capture the critical road and rail junction that was the city of Caen, bisected by the River Orne. The objectives of June 6 had not as yet been fully accomplished, even though the principal one—to become firmly established on the continent—had.

This first contest was undecided—dealing with the bulk of the German forces—as the Americans attacked Cherbourg, a port essential for the continuation of the Allied operations. Caen, which was supposed to fall on the evening of June 6, was still firmly in German hands, with the 21st Panzer Division and the 12th SS Panzer Division (Hitlerjugend) stubbornly preventing any frontal assault. But before the imminent arrival of Panzer Division Touraine (the British name for the Panzer Lehr Division), a flanking attack on Caen was still possible.

An attempt to encircle Caen from the west, via Tilly and Villers-Bocage, was common wisdom, but few were aware that Montgomery was planning an audacious raid to the east of the city.

Thanks to the in-depth accounts of British war diaries, the details of the aborted operation are still available today. In the War Diary of the Royal Scots Greys, an entry dated June 10 says that the battalion had to prepare for an attack the next day, under the auspices of the 4th Armoured Brigade, and to proceed to Bourguébus, via Cuverville and Demouville.

It was a prefiguration of Operation *Goodwood*, launched five weeks later with considerable numbers. The audacity of the plan was such that it required units to carry seven days' rations as lines of communication were at risk of disruption.

"Seawolf," a Centaur IV belonging to the Royal Marine Armoured Support Regiment. This was a rare tank, as only 80 are known to have been built. It is armed with an 85mm howitzer. The gradations painted onto the turret correspond to those of a compass, and allow an observer on foot to communicate the coordinates of an objective. (IWM H 37999)

# In Profile:
# Amphibious and Transport Vehicles

This M3 half-track belongs to one of the command posts—as evidenced by the presence of the SCR 609 radio post visible through the open right door/hatch—of one of three Tank Battalions of the 67th Armored Regiment, 2nd Armored Division. Strangely, this vehicle is not armed with a light .30-caliber Browning machine gun.

This GMC DUKW 353 2.5-ton 6x6 was deployed by the Royal Engineers, with the Royal Army Service Corps supplying the personnel. This amphibious vehicle is seen here with a tarpaulin cover, a common feature according to photographs taken in Normandy.

The "Portland Rose" was one of a number of GMC DUKW 353s used by the Allies to unload ships in the first days of the invasion. Rangers of the 5th Battalion at the Pointe du Hoc also used them. Later in the campaign, this amphibious vehicle was used for river crossings in the absence of bridges.

The Sherman Firefly was the only Allied tank able to destroy a Tiger in normal combat conditions, excepting the Challenger, which was far less common. This excellent example—the crew is having a cup of tea—is photographed among ruins that are actually English, not Norman: the scene played out ten days before the battle of Villers-Bocage, in a street in Portsmouth that was recently the victim of a Luftwaffe attack. (IWM H 35995)

But finally, on June 11, with the advance to the west of Caen having already begun the previous day, an order at 1500 hours annulled the 4th Armoured Brigade's operation, and the march on Bourguébus was halted. The brigade was needed to reinforce the 2nd Canadian Division in the Colomby–Villons-les-Buissons sector, where a Hitlerjugend counterattack loomed. The threat never materialized; the British realized this and did not give up on the operation, but the disaster at Villers-Bocage—where the British lost 53 armored vehicles to the 13 Tiger tanks of Lieutenant Michael Wittmann's 2nd Company, SS 101st Heavy Tank Battalion—forced a change in strategy that became the basis for, and origins of, Operation *Goodwood*.

# The Assault on Tilly

Launched on June 8, 1944, the attack on Tilly-sur-Seulles aimed to open the road to Villers-Bocage. To accomplish this, the British deployed the 8th Armoured Brigade and the 151st Infantry Brigade of the 50th Infantry Division. On the first day, results were satisfactory: the Wehrmacht 716th Infantry Division was incapable of challenging the advance and the British vanguard reached Saint-Pierre, a hamlet northeast of Tilly, nine kilometers from their starting line.

One of the "Bombe" codebreaking
machines at Bletchley Park.
(Magnus Manske)

Hut 6 Bletchley Park, as seen
today. It was here that the German
Enigma code was broken.
(Matt Crypto)

# In Profile: **Ultra**

In June 1941, "Ultra" became the generic term, the designation adopted by Stuart Menzies' British military intelligence for "sigint"—signals intelligence—harvested from breaking high-level encrypted enemy radio and teleprinter communications. This was in stark comparison to Admiral Wilhelm Canaris's Abwehr, German military intelligence, that relied primarily on one-dimensional "humint"—human intelligence—essentially spying.

Ultra was run through the Government Code and Cypher School (GC&CS) at Bletchley Park in Milton Keynes, Buckinghamshire. Ultra—from Ultra Secret, above even Most Secret or Top Secret—was to become the standard designation among the Allies for all such intelligence—excluding the USSR: Stalin was convinced, right up until the end of the war, that Britain and the United States would make a separate peace with Germany and turn on Russia and thus treated all Western intelligence with utmost scepticism. It was at Bletchley Park that the German Enigma and Lorenz ciphers were penetrated, providing the Allies with invaluable intelligence, from Luftwaffe strength in the Battle of Britain, Rommel's order of battle at El Alamein, Dönitz's U-boat inventory in the Atlantic, to Waffen-SS panzer dispositions in Normandy.

Working in Spartan conditions, with lack of heating in flimsy wooden huts, shabby food, poor sanitation—one toilet for 120 people, including women—and pitiful wages, the men and women at Bletchley worked long hours, driven only by a desire to defeat the enemy. Despised by the old guard but nurtured by Churchill, many were teenagers, barely out of school, but they were the brightest mathematical stars drawn from every sector of society, from Oxbridge, to government schools, to the post office.

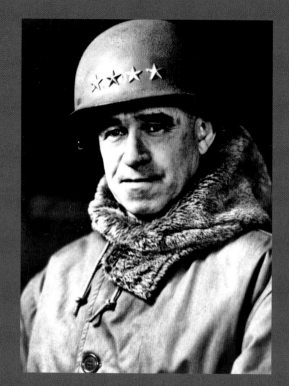

(U.S. Army)

# In Profile:
# Lieutenant General Omar Bradley

Bradley was born into a family of poverty-stricken sharecroppers in Missouri in 1893. Earning 17 cents an hour as a boilermaker, "Brad's" application to West Point was accepted in 1911. He graduated alongside Eisenhower in 1915 before serving on the Mexican border. Guarding copper mines in Montana, he was promoted captain and joined the 19th Infantry Division bound for the Western Front. However, the influenza epidemic intervened and the division was not deployed.

Between the wars, he studied infantry tactics, commanding the U.S. Army Infantry School at Fort Benning. In March 1942, he was promoted major general commanding the 82nd Infantry (later Airborne) Division. His first combat command was taking over Patton's II Corps after Operation *Torch* in Tunisia. He led II Corps in the invasion of Sicily.

In early 1944 he was transferred to London where he assumed command of the U.S. First Army, which, together with Dempsey's British Second Army, comprised Montgomery's 21st Army Group. During D-Day, he commanded three corps on the American beaches Utah and Omaha. He was responsible for formulating Operation *Cobra*, the successful breakout from the Normandy beachhead. Bradley's new command, the 12th Army Group, was to comprise four field armies of 43 divisions and 1.3 million troops. A solid, dependable general, Bradley was, however, overly cautious—at the Falaise Pocket he allowed some 50,000 Germans to escape—and although his command bore the brunt at the Battle of the Bulge, he was sidelined by Eisenhower in favour of Montgomery and Patton. Bradley was in the van in mid-April 1945 when he met the Soviets on the Elbe.

The next day, the battle configuration changed completely. The Panzer Lehr Division had arrived and General Fritz Bayerlein launched an immediate counterattack to retake Bayeux. The German advance was made ten kilometers to the west, exactly parallel to that of the British the previous day.

The two adversaries both threatened to encircle the town. The Germans, who had halted outside Arganchy to the north, were forced to veer off toward Tilly. At 1400 hours, they attacked in the direction of Chouain, Audrieu and Bucéels. Major von Schönberg-Waldenberg, commander of the 2nd Panzer Lehr Battalion, was killed during these attacks.

While this battle was taking place, Montgomery decided to reinforce his units: the 22nd Armoured Brigade (7th Armoured Division) attacked the next day, in the same sector, with Tilly and Hottot as the objective.

On June 19, the Germans renewed their attacks on Saint-Pierre and managed to dislodge the 8th Durham Light Infantry. But, in the face of the British advance, they could progress no further.

On the 22nd Armoured Brigade front, the advance began at 0630 hours. As was often the case during the battle of Normandy, its progress was significantly hampered by heavy traffic on the roads. It was not until 0755 hours that it made contact with the enemy at Bucéels (the brigade suffered its first casualties an hour later—to friendly fire).

As it was, the brigade had regrouped to begin the assault on Bucéels, the last village before Tilly. During this initial phase, several tank fights took place. The 4th County of London Yeomanry (CLY) claimed the destruction of a Panzer IV, while the 5th RTR was engaged in a more difficult fight: it lost two Cromwells that day, but claimed a Panther and an armored reconnaissance vehicle. It also captured a small German convoy comprising an ambulance and eight SdKfz 251 half-tracks.

At the end of the day, the 4th CLY and a company of Glosters captured Bucéels but the assault on Tilly ground to a halt. The battle of Tilly therefore ended in stalemate: the British were unable to take the town, while the Germans had failed in their attempt to recapture Bayeux.

## Desert Rats at Villers-Bocage

As the events of the battle of Tilly unfurled, the Americans, with the support of a single armored division, reached Caumont l'Eventé, 25 kilometers south of Bayeux, by the most direct route, and now posed a threat to the flanks of the Panzer Lehr. General Erskine, commander of the 7th Armoured Division, seized the opportunity to resume the attack in the direction of Villers-Bocage; a significant detour to the west of Tilly would provide them with a way around the bulk of the Panzer Lehr. It was an audacious move, but very much in the spirit of the Desert Rats.

On June 11, the division stalled outside Salmon, losing a Stuart, a Firefly and five Cromwells while only destroying four Panthers of the 1st Panzer Lehr Regiment. It was therefore with some relief that the tank crews learned that the division would, the next day, be attempting a large encircling movement, beginning at 1600 hours, and advancing toward Villers-Bocage via Jérusalem, Saint-Paul-de-Vernay, Livry and Amaye-sur-Seulles.

June 13, 1944 was decisive. It has been described *ad nauseam*, generally from the German point of view, but the reports contained in the British diaries offer an interesting perspective on the events.

A good starting point is the description of the battle of Villers-Bocage by the commander of the 22nd Armoured Brigade. As the reports arrived, piecemeal, by radio, they were written down in the unit's journal. The passages are therefore intensely dramatic, written as they were in the thick of the action and bubbling with emotion.

The advance on Villers-Bocage resumed at 0545 hours on June 13, 1944. The German opposition was weak and increasingly evanescent. At 0700 hours, local inhabitants questioned by the Allies implied that Villers-Bocage was being held by a single company of German infantry. The 22nd Armoured Brigade's war diary went something like this:

0800: The 4th CLY has entered the town, the residents say the enemy hold the chateau.

0830: 4th CLY Staff has been attacked and all their tanks destroyed.

0900: The brigadier has ordered the 1/7 Queens to enter the town and the 4th CLY to go to point 213. Reply: The road to point 213 is held by Tigers. Of the others established in the town, one of them was put out of action at 50 meters.

Three British tankmen taken prisoner by the Waffen SS being moved to the rear in a Kübelwagen. The insignia on the beret and the bands on the epaulettes, visible on another photograph on the same roll of film, identify these men as part of the Royal Tank Regiment. They were captured after their tank was destroyed by Wittmann's company. (Bundesarchiv 497/3506A/9A)

A half-track destroyed by Wittman outside Villers-Bocage. (IWM)

1115: The 4th CLY indicate that the situation in town is absolutely untenable due to fire from 88mms.

1235: The 4th CLY signal that 5 Tigers in town and a 6th outside it are trying to surround the lead squadron and soon after the commander of the 4th CLY says that he has been surrounded and asks for a smokescreen as cover.

1240: He asks for the authorization to scuttle his scout car. Granted.

1525: The head of the 1/7 Queens asks for more infantry as enemy infiltrations into V-B are multiplying.

1600: The 1/5 Queens receive the order to reinforce V-B.

1650: The head of the brigade warns the division commander that the situation in untenable. The latter accepts the abandonment of V-B but gives the order to hold on to the high places at all costs.

Day's losses:

- 5th Royal Tank Regiment: 1 Cromwell;

- 4th CLY: 13 Cromwell IVs, 3 Cromwells, 2 Cromwell VIs, 3 Stuarts, 4 Sherman Fireflies (being 26 tanks in total);

- 1st Rifle Brigade: 14 Half-tracks, 8 Bren Carriers, 8 Lloyd Carriers.

The setback at Villers-Bocage put a temporary stop to the British attempts to make a quick breakthrough before their planned capture of Caen. To achieve that objective, it would take a lot of effort, time and patience, and for this the coming operation would have to be carefully planned.

# In Profile:
# British Tanks

T 271938

T 271938

One of the 11th Armoured Division's Cromwell tanks, on July 17, at Flers. The registration numbers and codes have been painted on; "Jean" is possibly one of the crew's girlfriends.

A Challenger from the 11th Armoured Division at Flers on July 17, 1944. The triangular marking (opposite page) suggests that the tank belongs to A Squadron. Only a few Challengers were deployed in Normandy.

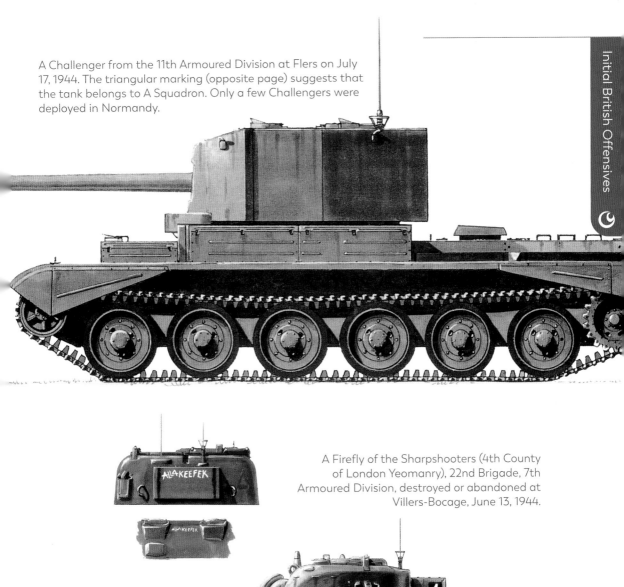

A Firefly of the Sharpshooters (4th County of London Yeomanry), 22nd Brigade, 7th Armoured Division, destroyed or abandoned at Villers-Bocage, June 13, 1944.

The 17-pounder gun, firing armor-piercing discarding sabot (APDS) projectiles, was the most fearsome weapon used on the field of battle, even compared with the Tiger II's offering. Only the Tiger's armor allowed it to engage, at a distance, with tanks carrying these guns.

# *Epsom* Preparation

At first sight, Operation *Epsom* was nothing but a repetition of the maneuver made by the 7th Armoured Division and stopped by Wittmann's 2nd Company, SS 101st Heavy Tank Battalion Tigers. The objective was the same: Caen. The method of reaching it was the same: hooking in from the west before veering off to the Vaucelles neighborhood to the south. But while the scope of *Epsom* was smaller, the means were far more powerful: VIII Corps would deliver the principal attack with two infantry divisions (15th Scottish and 43rd Wessex), two independent armored brigades (31st Tank and 4th Armoured), and an armored division (11th Armoured)—over 600 tanks and 300 artillery pieces in total.

The main attack would also be supported to the west with assaults by the 49th West Riding Division and the 8th Armoured Division, who had to seize the heights of Rauray. Nearer Caen, it was the II Canadian Corps that would protect the VIII Corps' flanks, while the 51st Highland Division was ready, if needed, to close the pincers at the paratroopers' bridgehead, east of the Orne.

More than being purely territorial in nature, Montgomery's ultimate goal for the operation was to draw the bulk of the German armored divisions to the British front, leaving the Americans free to take Cherbourg and then launch a decisive attack toward the south relatively unimpeded.

At the same time, Rommel was planning a massed panzer offensive in the Caumont sector, at the junction of the Americans and the British. The first to attack would have a considerable advantage over the other, achieving with one move the strategic ascendancy over his adversary and the disruption of the latter's plans. Thanks to Ultra, which allowed the

A Cromwell IV from the general staff of the 11th Armoured Division in Normandy. (IWM)

An outstanding photograph of a rare tank—the Achilles, a British tank destroyer based on the chassis of the American M10, but armed with a 17-pounder that was altogether more powerful than the 75mm piece on the American TD. "Glengarry II" is about to engage in the battles of the Odon. (IWM)

Allies to read the Germans' encoded messages, Montgomery was forewarned of Rommel's threatened attack and hurried along his preparations accordingly. When he attacked at dawn on June 25, he completely surprised the Germans.

Yet despite their obvious numerical advantage, the British suffered a handicap very real yet rarely discussed: inexperience. While the landings had mostly been accomplished by seasoned troops like the 13/18 Hussars (who had already fought in France, in 1939), Operation *Epsom* was carried out by men who, for the most part, had not experienced combat before. Only the 4th Armoured Brigade had fought before, in North Africa and then in Italy.

On the German side, the Panzer Lehr and the 12th SS Panzer Division (Hitlerjugend) were elite divisions, combat experienced before the landings, with two weeks of hard fighting since, and were at the time perfectly honed and ready.

# June 26: VIII Corps Attacks

The previous day, General Horrocks's XXX Corps had launched an offensive in the Rauray sector. They did not achieve all their objectives—far from it—but at least the enemy was fixed in this region while General O'Connor's VII Corps was preparing to attack.

Thanks to the support of their neighboring corps, some 800 artillery pieces opened fire on June 26 at 0730 hours. Naval guns also took part, with monitors *Erebus* and *Roberts* and the battleship HMS *Rodney* adding to the cacophony.

The British offensive started well. While the first day of combat was somewhat restrained, Montgomery's forces had only just started, and the attack was renewed with the same vigor the next day.

On June 27, the 11th Armoured Division's effort toward the Odon got under way, and was rewarded at 1730 hours when the 23 Hussars' Shermans, accompanied by the infantry of the 2nd Argyll & Sutherlands, managed to seize intact a bridge over the river at Tourville.

## The Push Toward the Odon

The new bridgehead was immediately utilized. As night brought a certain respite, the 29th Armoured Brigade toll demonstrated the intensity of the fighting. Nineteen men had been killed, two were missing and 61 were injured, two of whom were officers. Of the recorded 121 Sherman IIs, 19 had been put out of action, three were lightly damaged, and four others had been damaged and repaired the same day. Despite the return of one Firefly, five Fireflies were destroyed, leaving the brigade with thirty-one. It was among the Stuarts that the losses were, proportionately, the highest: 11 destroyed and three damaged. Eighteen remained. In total, the brigade had 170 tanks ready for action at dawn on June 28.

But the losses had not been in vain: the brigade posted a very respectable scorecard itself, taking out four Tigers (three of which were destroyed), 12 Panthers (11 destroyed), three Panzer IVs (one destroyed), and one self-propelled gun destroyed and three out of action, plus nine other guns put out of action (all belonging to the Hitlerjugend, except the Tigers).

This Churchill infantry tank—a Mark IV—is from the 7th Royal Tank Regiment, 31st Armoured Brigade, accompanied by infantry of the 15th Scottish Infantry Division, during Operation *Epsom*, June 28, 1944. (IWM)

# More and More Panzers

June 28 was a rainy day, and only a few reconnaissance aircraft took to the air. These intrepid craft discovered behind the front two newly arrived panzer divisions—the 9th SS Panzer Division (Hohenstaufen) and 10th SS Panzer Division (Frundsberg) of the II SS Panzer Corps—which were surely going to engage in the battle. Montgomery's plan was, then, working well regarding one of his objectives: to draw as many German tanks as possible to the east of the bridgehead.

The two original panzer divisions, the Panzer Lehr and the Hitlerjugend, were no longer able to resist the Allies alone. The back-up provided by the SS 101st Heavy Tank Battalion was not enough, and a battle group made up of the 2nd SS Panzer Division (Das Reich) was therefore also engaged. To the west, in the Rauray sector, the Das Reich held the extremity of the battlefield, while to the east, the 21st Panzer Division was launching probing attacks to try to distract the British forces engaged in the corridor of the Odon. Thus, five German armored divisions were directly engaged against the 11th Armoured Division and the two independent brigades. The threat that the British attack posed to the entire German front was made apparent when the II SS Panzer Corps was committed to battle as soon as it arrived in Normandy.

The battle continued to rage on the banks of the Odon, the British managing to enlarge their bridgehead to the south of the river by seizing a new bridge at Gavrus, some elements arriving at the summit of Hill 112, where they retired for the evening. In the 29th Armoured Brigade, 17 had died, two were missing and 48 had been wounded in the battle. Tank losses were light, as most vehicles hit were only damaged. Therefore, on the evening of the 28th, the brigade had 123 battle-ready Sherman IIs (two more than the previous day), 25 Fireflies (six fewer) and 17 Stuarts (instead of 18): in total, 165 compared to 170 on the 27th. In fact, 20 tanks had been put out of action, but the repair workshops had worked hard through the night to restore a large proportion of the damaged vehicles.

The brigade claimed the destruction of three Tigers, a Panzer IV and two Panthers, as well as an antitank gun and two field guns. Three other tanks and two guns were put out of action.

The fighting that raged on the right bank of the Odon should not eclipse that which took place to the north of the river. In effect, the Germans still held the southern access of Grainville-sur-Odon, threatening by the same token the entire bridgehead of VIII Corps. To counter this, the 9th RTR and its Churchills resumed the interrupted assault of the previous day. Fighting unfolded around and in Grainville throughout the day. Two Panthers were destroyed, as was a Churchill. On this occasion, the officer responsible for the battalion's war diary wrote happily of the robustness of the Churchill, saying it resisted antitank fire well, and when it caught fire it burned slowly and the crew had every chance to escape. In contrast, the Panthers had a tendency to explode.

The Scots Greys left their sector on June 28 to approach the Odon where, the next day, they found themselves in support of 129th Infantry Brigade.

# In Profile:
# American Shermans

An M4A3 Sherman from an unidentified American unit in Normandy during July 1944. The olive-drab paint looks worn. Regimental workshops increasingly applied irregular, darker brown or green stripes to the Shermans of the 2nd Armored Division, for better camouflage.

This M4 Sherman belongs to one of the units allocated Sherman Duplex Drives that adopted the large British numbers painted on the turret or flanks.

"Bachelor Boys" is an American M3 Sherman from an unidentified unit that has, at some risk, kept its highly visible American markings from the start of the campaign.

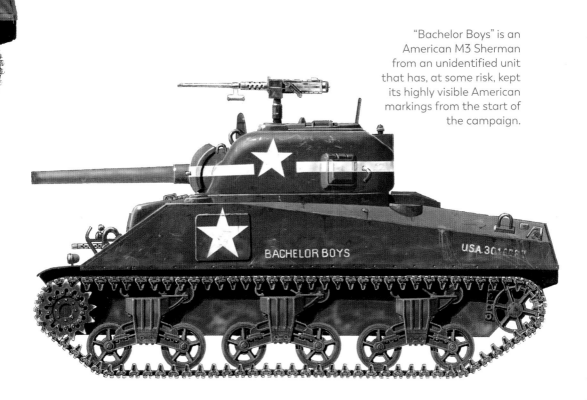

# General Battle

On June 29, the British reinforced their positions, notably in their bridgehead south of the Odon. In this spirit the 129th Infantry Brigade and the Scots Greys were deployed along the Gavrus–Fontaine Etoupefour road. This sector was cleared of most enemy elements. In the west, however, where XXX Corps had not managed to advance satisfactorily, the flank of the so-called "Scottish corridor" was exposed. It was evidently here that the II SS Panzer Corps would attack, with the 9th and 10th SS Panzer Divisions. The Frundsberg would fix the British at Hill 112, while the Hohenstaufen would press on to Grainville and Cheux.

The German task was problematic, as the British had amassed almost 500 tanks in the small salient. In addition, after several days of bad weather, the skies had cleared and in the morning, the 2nd Tactical Air Force appeared over the battlefield, causing significant losses among the German assailants still in the process of deploying. Over 250 vehicles were destroyed or put out of action. In the early afternoon, the Hohenstaufen seized Grainville, but could not make any progress toward Cheux—where some isolated Panthers were easily stopped in their tracks—or toward the hamlet of Colleville, held by the 9th RTR with their Churchills.

According to the 9th RTR war diary, no panzers appeared outside the village, though an infantry attack was swept aside by machine-gun fire from the Churchills' Besa machine guns. The tank crews claimed that they had annihilated an entire infantry battalion but 9th SS Panzer Division lost no more than 150 men that day. As night fell, the British retook Grainville.

At Gavrus, the Frundsberg tried to eliminate the southernmost point of the Scottish advance of the preceding days, clashing ferociously with the 2nd Argylls in the attempt. All day, the 10th SS Panzer Division tanks were held in check outside the village, both by Scottish artillery and by the threat of the PIATs. The defense was mounted by Major William McElwee, an unwarlike reservist and historian specializing in the 17th century.

By the day's end, the 2nd Argylls could no longer hold on and were forced to retreat several hundred meters, but still holding the bridges over the Odon at Gavrus. The 29th Armoured Brigade (11th Armoured Division) had absorbed the main enemy assault. Losses were much heavier than the preceding days', with 18 dead, 20 missing and 114 wounded. With 150 tanks available at the end of the day, compared to 165 24 hours earlier, the brigade remained at a reasonable strength, especially since the division's workshops had said they would be able to repair 26 tanks by the next day.

# The Counterattack Falters

For the British defenders, night brought but short respite, as the Germans renewed their assault at 0130 hours in an attempt to avoid the devastating fire from Allied aircraft that would surely happen in the morning. For Battle Group Hohenstaufen, the attack was doomed from the start, with the young SS stormtroopers failing to achieve any of their objectives.

A Sherman II (M4A2) from the 11th Armoured Division, with a group of soldiers from the 3rd Infantry Division on top. The extra radio antenna attached to the ventilator suggests this is a command tank. (IWM)

As for the 10th SS Panzer Division, it retook Hill 112 and established a firm hold on its prize.

But the battle had already lost its intensity. The best evidence of this was that the 11th Armoured Division was relieved the next day. The 154 tanks of the 29th Armoured Brigade were therefore not needed to contain the Germans; in fact, it seemed that it was the British infantry, supported by aviation and artillery, that would occupy the attentions of the panzer divisions attacking the salient. This was a clear indication of the confidence invested in the infantry by the Allied command. The 4th Armoured stayed put in the Scottish Corridor, but it barely intervened at all on June 30 and July 1, and most of its units were simply held in reserve.

On July 1, the Germans launched their final offensive, but their hearts were no longer in the fight. C Squadron, 24th Lancers stopped a handful of Panthers at Rauray, in a fight that was to typify the closing stages of the Odon battle. Four Panthers were surprised at about 800 meters by British Shermans. Apparently they did not suspect that any Allied tanks might be in the sector. The C Squadron, 24th Lancers war diary records that one Panther was put out of action and caught fire immediately, being hit in the side armor between the tracks and the underside of the chassis. A Panther emerged at around 1,000 meters, following the same path as the previous four tanks. It was also engaged, but not hit. Its reaction was to advance very slowly and to finally stop behind a tree that offered neither camouflage nor protection. It was then hit in the front by several antitank shells, but without result.

## Assessing the First Massive Offensive

For Montgomery, the balance sheet for Operation *Epsom* was ambivalent. The breakthrough came up short: Caen was still in German hands. From this viewpoint, the operation was a failure. But there was more to worry about: from a tactical point of view, the armored

A battery from a medium artillery regiment in the Noman *bocage*, June 13, 1944. The rapid deployment of these 4.5-inch field guns, without preparing the ground or using specific camouflage, typifies the intensity of the first days of the campaign. Just visible in the background are radio vehicles of the Royal Corps of Signals, detached to the batteries of the Royal Artillery Corps. (IWM)

brigades had shown that they were incapable of penetrating enemy territory with any significance: what was five kilometers, after all? And yet, at least during the first two days of combat, the British had a considerable advantage in numbers.

The strategic lessons were more encouraging: throughout the offensive, every single panzer division in Normandy had thus far been engaged against the British. During this time, the Americans had only encountered one division of panzergrenadiers equipped with assault guns. Therefore, the plan to draw the bulk of the German armored corps into a fight against the British was an undeniable success. In addition, the arrival of the whole of II SS Panzer Corps suggested that the Germans had no more reserves in the west: they were now forced to call on units still needed for the Eastern Front.

Finally, added to those of the previous weeks, the losses suffered by the Germans during Operation *Epsom* were heavy. On average, the panzer divisions had lost around 100 tanks a week. The 300 panzers of the II SS Panzer Corps could not fill the lacuna: at such a rate the panzer divisions would cease to exist in less than six more weeks.

Allied losses were moderate. The 29th Armoured Brigade, 11th Armoured Division, provides a typical tally: on the eve of battle, it had 154 Sherman IIs, 36 Sherman VC Fireflies and 33 Stuarts. On July 1, after five days of combat, it still had 131 Sherman IIs, 26 Sherman VC Fireflies and 20 Stuarts. This means that the brigade lost 23 Sherman IIs, 10 Fireflies and 13 Stuarts—46 tanks in all. It claimed the destruction of 34 panzers over the same period, most of which were attributed to the Fireflies. Finally, just 78 men lost their lives.

The division was therefore virtually intact and ready to resume the offensive in a few days, when reinforcements arrived. The Germans, however, would never recoup the losses they suffered during *Epsom*.

An M10 tank destroyer in a Saint-Lô street on July 24, 1944, the eve of Operation *Cobra*. The vehicle has been covered with planks and sandbags to avoid the deadly German panzerfausts, widely used by the Germans in the *bocage*. (National Archives)

# Caen: From Stalemate to Breakthrough

While the British were exerting maximum pressure to the east of the bridgehead, the Americans were mobilizing their own armored units on the Cotentin Peninsula.

Priority had been given to the infantry: nine divisions had landed in June, not including the two airborne divisions. The first complete U.S. armored division in Normandy was the 2nd Armored, a heavy division. The first elements embarked in the morning of June 6, 1944, to arrive off Omaha Beach in the evening. During the night, an LST hit a mine, exploded and sank, taking with it 17 Shermans and 14 Stuarts.

The bulk of the division landed on June 9. The divisional commander, Major General Edward H. Brooks, landed on June 11, and on June 14 the two most important elements arrived: the Combat Commands. On June 28, they were joined by the service and logistical elements; the division was fully constituted on the evening of July 2.

Once in Normandy, the division was divided into two Combat Commands of roughly equal size, with a reserve of a tank battalion and an infantry battalion. Outside of its normal composition, the division was allocated supplementary units such as the 82nd Reconnaissance Battalion, 195th Antiaircraft Battalion and the 702nd Tank Destroyer Battalion.

Lieutenant-General Miles Dempsey, commanding British Second Army, with General Montgomery in France, July 16, 1944. (Sgt Morris, No. 5 Army Film & Photographic Unit / IWM B 7405)

# In Profile:
# Lieutenant-General Miles Dempsey

General Sir Miles Christopher Dempsey, GBE, KCB, DSO, MC was born in Cheshire, England in 1896. He graduated from the Royal Military College, Sandhurst in 1915 and was commissioned, at 17, into the Royal Berkshire Regiment, a Regular Army unit of the BEF, He saw action at Delville Wood, part of the Somme offensive in 1916, and the following year at Miraumont, Oppy and at the battle of Cambrai. During the German Spring Offensive of March 1918, Dempsey, OC D Company, was wounded in a mustard-gas attack and evacuated to England where he had a lung removed. He returned to the front in July and took part in the Allied Hundred Days Offensive.

Between the wars he served with his regiment in India and Persia, before attending Staff College, Camberley. After a stint as brigade major 5th Infantry Brigade, September 1939 found him as a half-colonel commanding 1st Battalion Royal Berkshires. Promoted to brigadier in 1940, at just 42, his 13th Infantry Brigade distinguished itself in the rear-guard action at Dunkirk, but suffered an 85-percent casualty rate.

In December 1942 Dempsey took command of XIII Corps, Eighth Army in North Africa and led his corps in the July 1943 invasion of Sicily and the invasion of Italy. He commanded the Anglo-Canadian Second Army at D-Day on the beaches of Sword, Juno and Gold, his troops subsequently heavily involved in the fighting around Caen. With Bradley, he facilitated Operation *Cobra*, the breakout from Normandy. The Second Army liberated Brussels and Antwerp and was reluctantly involved in the disastrous Operation *Market Garden*. On March 23, 1945, Dempsey became the first British Army commander to cross the Rhine.

In addition, the organization of the 67th Armored Regiment was slightly amended with the previous split into two battalions of medium tanks and light tanks abandoned, ill-suited, it was felt, to modern warfare. Each battalion, as in the light divisions, thus had two companies of medium tanks and one of light tanks, allowing a better distribution of M5s.

During the deployment of the 2nd Armored Division, the Americans used the tanks attached to their infantry divisions to overcome German resistance.

## American Tanks at Quinéville

Two armored battalions engaged in the operations at Cherbourg: the 70th and 746th Tank Battalions, under the umbrella of the 6th Armored Group led by Colonel Francis F. Fainter.

From June 6 to 8, the Americans consolidated their bridgehead around Utah Beach and Sainte-Mère-Église, but did not attempt to break out until June 9, when the 8th Infantry Division moved north.

The first attempts failed in the face of stiff resistance posed by the German, notably elements of the 709th Infantry Division reinforced by troops from the 243rd Infantry

377th Antiaircraft Battalion troops firing quadruple 12.7mm guns in a ground role. The unit was attached to the 4th U.S. Infantry Division, and landed on Utah Beach on June 6 before taking the Montebourg–Quinéville line during the first week of the Normandy campaign. (National Archives)

# In Profile:
# British Shermans

This Sherman belongs to C Squadron, 17/18 Hussars (indicated by the white 51 on a red square), 27th Independent Armoured Brigade (indicated by the seahorse insignia). Nicknamed "Cavalier," this Firefly is armed with a 75mm gun.

*Opposite and left:* This Sherman VC Firefly is the second tank of Troop 1, A Squadron, East Riding Yeomanry, the junior regiment of the 27th Armoured Brigade.

A Sherman VC Firefly—possibly
from the 13/18 Hussars—that
landed during the early days of the
Normandy campaign. The large
number (71) painted on the turret
could indicate that this tank
is armed with a 17-pounder.

A street in Isigny during the first week of the Normandy campaign. In one week, the Americans landed a total of 12,000 vehicles and 86,000 men on Utah Beach. (IWM OWIL 31075)

Division and Sturm Battalion AOK 7 (Armeeoberkommando 7) who had come from Cherbourg on bicycles. Armed with Nebelwerfers and 88mm guns, they held the critical crossroads and roads leading north.

Held in check all day around Ecausseville and a huge dirigible hangar, the 8th Infantry appealed to the tanks for help, and at the end of the day, the 1st Battalion attacked on the right flank with the help of two sections of Shermans from A Company, 70th Tank Battalion.

The Shermans led the way, crossing the streams that had caused so much trouble for the infantry and firing on the village of Ecausseville, where the 88s responded in kind. The American tanks then about-faced and rejoined the infantry, before seizing a hamlet where around a hundred prisoners were taken. During the night, the Germans abandoned Ecauseville, now too exposed, and returned to the sector of Montebourg and its railway station.

On June 10, the Americans resumed their advance northward, the 1st Battalion accompanied as ever by medium tanks, on which the infantry rode. About 500 meters from Eroudeville, German fire forced the troops to dismount, but the tanks continued and put three Pak guns out of action.

The infantry followed and, after a violent struggle, they managed to seize the village. At around 1300 hours, Sturm Battalion AOK 7 counterattacked and drove the Americans back several hundred meters. Tanks were called in to respond, but stopping the Germans was no easy feat: it took the Shermans five attempts to retake Eroudeville.

(U.S. Army Center
for Military History)

# In Profile:
# Lieutenant General
# Courtney Hodges

Courtney Hicks Hodges was born in 1887 in Perry, Georgia. After a spell at agricultural college, he enrolled at West Point but dropped out after just a year, being "found deficient" in mathematics. In 1906 he enlisted in the army as a private, and quickly rose through the ranks, receiving his commission in 1909 as a second lieutenant, serving with George Marshall in the Philippines and George Patton in Mexico.

During World War I on the Western Front, he was decorated for heroism—the Distinguished Service Cross—for leading his battalion of the 6th Infantry Regiment, 5th Division in an attack across the River Marne. After the war he became an instructor at West Point before being appointed commandant U.S. Army Infantry School at Fort Benning. He was promoted

major general in 1941, taking command of X Corps and then Third Army before being sent to England where he served as Bradley's First Army deputy during Operation *Overlord*, the Allied invasion of Normandy.

In August 1944 he assumed command of First Army, his troops being among the first to reach Paris. Diverted to the Ardennes, First Army saw action in the attritional battles of the Bulge, Aachen and Hurtgen Forest, before capturing the Ludendorff Bridge across the Rhine at Remagen. Regarded by Eisenhower as the "spearhead and scintillating star" of the U.S. advance into Germany, Hodges, after Walter Kreuger, was the second soldier in U.S. history to progress from private to four-star general. He died in 1966 in San Antonio, Texas.

On June 11, the American advance continued and the village of Ham fell, while the first elements of the 8th Infantry Regiment reached the railway station at Montebourg. American progress, hampered by defiant resistance, was slow. Along the coast, Quinéville still held.

The 12th Infantry Regiment was deployed between Montebourg station and Quinéville. It had also suffered during its advance north, before calling on the tanks of the 746th Tank Battalion to overcome problematic German strongpoints, notably on June 8, to take the Château de Dodinville, near Joganville, where six B Company Shermans were engaged.

On June 11, attempts to take Montebourg failed, and the Germans counterattacked yet again.

A self-propelled M7 Priest in action in the *bocage*. The "war of the hedgerows" was far costlier for the Americans than the fighting on the open plains around Caen was for the British. (IWM EA 44239)

# Assault on Quinéville

The American offensive, north along the coast, was entrusted to the 22nd Infantry Regiment, who lost several days fixed by enemy artillery defending Crisbecq and Azeville. After the eventual fall of Azeville, General Barber formed a Task Force charged with skirting Crisbecq to seize Quinéville and the heights that towered over the village, which had been heavily fortified by the Germans. This Task Force was composed of the 22nd Infantry Battalion, the 899th Tank Battalion with its M10s, and the 746th Tank Battalion, and took the name of its commander, Brigadier General Barber.

The plan was that the Task Force would advance north, untroubled by the Crisbecq battery that would be preoccupied with the artillery of the 4th U.S. Division. The German escape corridor would be monitored by the tank destroyers and infantry just in case the enemy attempted a sortie to attack Task Force Barber's flank. For three days—June 10–12—the Task Force was unable to make any progress, as bad weather prevented the intervention of any aerial support. The presence of tanks didn't help at all, and it seemed that the infantry, which had already suffered greatly since June 6, was just hanging on; L Company, 22nd Battalion had already lost 159 men in the five days since the landings.

The VII Corps commander, General J. Lawton Collins, therefore decided to commit the 39th Infantry Regiment, 9th Division, which had just arrived in Normandy, on June 11.

On the morning of June 12, the regiment attacked, found the Crisbecq battery abandoned and pursued the Germans north. During this time, the 22nd Battalion also resumed its offensive northward, supported by a section of tanks from C Company, 70th Tank Battalion. Two artillery battalions also supported the advance, as did a naval bombardment of Quinéville. The village of Ozeville was soon captured—the last line of defense before Quinéville.

On June 14, with the support of the 70th Tank Battalion, the 22nd Infantry prepared for the assault on Quinéville. It was further supported by a battalion of the 39th Infantry. The tanks, observing vehicles moving in the distance, fired on the targets, which quickly retreated. These were, in fact, American tank destroyers.

The first American elements that penetrated Quinéville were easily repelled by Germans solidly established in a series of bunkers situated along the beach and at the mouth of the Sinope. The Mont Coquerel battery, however, was irrelevant, as it was directed seaward.

A Cromwell from the Armoured Reconnaissance Regiment, Guards Armoured Division, identifiable from its 45 code. The Guards went through their baptism of fire during Operation *Goodwood*. (IWM H 37171)

# In Profile:
# American Shermans

An M4 Sherman from a sub-unit of the 4th U.S. Armored Division, at Pontaubault, at the end of July 1944. Its stars have been covered in darker paint.

An M4A1 Sherman, nicknamed "Sherry", from an unidentified American unit. The white stars have already been painted over.

This M4A3 Sherman, nicknamed "Hurricane," from H Company has instead been camouflaged with streaks of brown paint.

99

An American gunner near Saint-Lô examines a destroyed German self-propelled Marder that probably blew up having taken a direct hit. (National Archives)

A second attempt to storm Quinéville failed; three Shermans made it to the central crossroads, but the first was damaged by a Pak gun firing from the beach, while the others encountered an antitank obstacle that was impossible to cross. The tanks were forced to withdraw.

In late afternoon, artillery of the 4th U.S. Division fired smoke to cover the American infantry as they stormed the streets, reaching the German casemates. The entire garrison surrendered and by 2130 hours, the Americans were the new masters of Quinéville.

The first week of fighting in the Cotentin therefore ended on a high note for the Americans. The German resistance had been far stronger than anticipated, but never strong enough to attack the bridgehead in force, and from June 6 to June 14, no fewer than 86,000 men, 12,000 vehicles and 26,000 tons of matériel landed on Utah Beach.

It had been difficult for the Americans to use tanks because of the nature of the terrain: the *bocage* country—tight-packed hedgerows—prevented any attempt to break through the

American infantry advances south through Saint-Lô, Périers and Lessay the day after the launch of Operation *Cobra*. (IWM EA 31082)

enemy lines. Tanks therefore only intervened to support infantry in overcoming stubborn German resistance. In this sense, the British were more audacious in their tank missions during the early stages of the campaign.

# Armored Divisions Prepare

The 2nd Armored Division's first notable action took place on June 12, in the Carentan sector, just as the 17th SS Panzergrenadier Division (Götz von Berlichingen) arrived.

Four Shermans were lost, but the paratroopers of the 101st Airborne needed no help in taking their sector and, for the weeks that followed, the division remained in reserve. Most of the fighting in the American sector took place in the Cotentin Peninsula, objective number one being the transatlantic port of Cherbourg.

After the peninsula had been cut off in mid-June, American infantry advanced on Cherbourg, which fell on June 30, when the 2nd Armored Division received the order to relieve the British 7th Armoured in the Caumont sector. It stayed there until mid-July, preparing for Operation *Cobra*.

The other American armored divisions had similar experiences over this period. The 3rd Armored completed its landings on July 9, and the 4th and 6th on July 28. But the infantry did not fight alone; during the violent clashes at Sainteny, from July 4–11: the 83rd Infantry Division was supported by the Shermans of the 746th Tank Battalion and the M10s of the 802nd Tank Destroyer Battalion.

As for the 4th Infantry Division, it was backed by the 70th Tank Battalion and the 801st Tank Destroyer Battalion.

In contrast, during the Panzer Lehr's counterattack at the Vire–Taute canal, the 30th Infantry Division received the not inconsiderable help of Combat Command B, 3rd Armored Division to stop Bayerlein's force.

"Derby," a tank belonging to D Company, 32nd Armoured Regiment, 3rd Armoured Division, alongside the remains of a Panzer IV from the 2nd SS Panzer Division Das Reich. The two infantrymen are from an 81mm mortar team. (National Archives)

After the capture of Saint-Lô, the critical junction at the heel of the Cotentin, the American forces were given a ten-day break to prepare for Operation *Cobra*.

The U.S. armored divisions were thus concentrated to deliver an unprecedented *coup de main* against a German front that was both weakened and deprived of any reinforcements due to Montgomery's unrelenting pounding of the Caen sector.

## Assault on Caen

The battle of the Odon ended on July 2, 1944. As soon as it was over, the Panzer Lehr Division was transferred to the American sector, while initial elements of the SS Das Reich also appeared. For Montgomery, the lesson was clear: if he left the slightest opening on the eastern front of the bridgehead, German armor would take advantage of it. He therefore had to persist in his attacks in the Caen sector until the Americans were ready.

Caen was a symbol of something much bigger: it had been among the objectives on June 6, but a month had passed since then and it was still in German hands.

In the end, a frontal assault was chosen for the attack on Caen, and not without reason: all envelopment attempts so far had failed. Even if the Allies only managed to advance five kilometers, as they had during *Epsom*, it would be enough to take Caen.

Nevertheless, a preliminary operation was necessary to reduce the German defenses at Carpiquet, which threatened the flank of the proposed offensive.

Operation *Windsor* was, above all, a Canadian affair, and was launched on July 4 by the 3rd Canadian Infantry Division and elements of the 2nd Canadian Armoured Brigade, notably the 10th Armoured Regiment (Fort Garry Horse), alongside the division's 141st Regiment Royal Armoured Corps, equipped with Churchill flamethrowers.

The attack began with a textbook bombardment, which provoked a swift reaction from the Hitlerjugend division holding Carpiquet and its aerodrome. The Canadians suffered significant losses as they mobilized in woods near Marcelet. When the assault was unleashed, the North Shore Regiment and the Régiment de la Chaudière managed to seize the village of Carpiquet, but they could not extend their reach to the airfield, where a handful of men from the 1st Battalion, 26th Panzergrenadier Regiment was entrenched.

When the Fort Garry Horse Shermans approached in support, they were attacked by an 88mm battery and were forced to stop.

By a curious paradox, the German general staff had actually considered Carpiquet lost since midday July 6, when some fifty SS troopers were still hanging on and the Canadians were informing Montgomery that the airfield was nowhere near being captured.

In the shelter of a hedge on the outskirts of Marigny, self-propelled 75mm M8 howitzers prepare to fire on German positions. The M8 in the foreground is equipped with a Culin hedge-cutter. (National Archives)

Finally, Operation *Charnwood*, the assault on Caen, was launched, though the Carpiquet aerodrome was still held by the Germans. On the evening of July 7, 2,200 tons of bombs were dropped on the German lines, pulverizing the northern sector of Caen but leaving the German front intact. The next morning, three infantry divisions were launched against positions held by the Hitlerjugend and the 16th Luftwaffe Field Division. The operation had got off to a promising start, especially for the 3rd British Infantry Division, who overran the Luftwaffe soldiers with some ease.

But in the center, the 59th Infantry Division, recently landed in Normandy, was stopped by volunteers from the Hitlerjugend at La Bijude. The hamlet changed hands twice in a matter of hours.

To the west, however, the Canadians, supported by the Shermans of the Sherbrooke Fusiliers, made good inroads, so that the two flanking divisions of the Allied offensive met in the middle at Caen, encircling the bulk of the Hitlerjugend in the process. To escape impending doom, Maj-Gen Kurt Meyer ordered his men to retreat south of the Orne, thus surrendering most of Caen to the Allies.

This withdrawal, contradicting the orders of the German staff, saved the division. It was carried out at night, on July 9/10, while Allied progress was being hampered by the ruins from their incessant bombardments. In the small hours of the morning on July 10, the last bridges over the Orne were blown up and the front was stabilized, with the Allies to the north and in the center of Caen, and the Germans clinging to the southern suburb of Vaucelles.

## Operation *Jupiter*

The capture of Caen did not signal the end of operations in the eastern zone of the bridgehead—far from it.

Montgomery gave the Germans no respite, as on July 10 he launched a new offensive, *Jupiter*, in the Hill 112 sector, where Operation *Epsom* had ended a month earlier. The British objective, other than the recapture of Hill 112, was to reach the Orne so it could set its front along the river.

The principal reason for this admittedly secondary assault, however, was to fix the II SS Panzer Corps on the British front. On July 8, the Panzer Lehr had launched a counterattack in the American sector. Though it was easily extinguished, the attack could not be allowed to resume with the arrival of fresh armored divisions, so it was necessary to keep the 9th and 10th SS Panzer Divisions occupied to the southwest of Caen.

To accomplish this, the Allies sent the 43rd Infantry Division into action, reinforced by the 46th (Scottish) Brigade and two armored brigades, the 4th Armoured and the 31st Tank. Against them, the front was held by the entire II SS Panzer Corps: the 9th SS Panzer Division (Hohenstaufen), 10th SS Panzer Division (Frundsberg) and the SS 101st Heavy Tank Battalion

The attack began on July 10 and lasted for two days, with no significant breakthroughs or changes to the front.

# The Americans Look for a Starting Line

After the first six weeks of action in Normandy, the Americans were no longer content with playing what they saw as a secondary role—at least, when compared to the British effort—in the campaign. But U.S. infantry operations in the *bocage*, first toward Cherbourg and then to Saint-Lô, had cost the Americans heavier losses than those suffered by the British engaged in their tank battles.

American casualties amounted to 22,000 in the battle of Cherbourg, and 40,000 more during the offensive at Saint-Lô. Over the same period, British losses amounted to 34,700 men in total. The Germans, by July 17, had lost 100,000 men—a figure marginally higher than the Allied total—the difference being that Rommel himself admitted that only six percent of the losses had been made up as of July 12, when the Allies were almost back to full complement.

After the capture of Saint-Lô, the Americans called a ten-day hiatus to gear up their war machine. Now that they had a solid, hard-won starting position, away from the swamps that had hampered their progress up until that point, they could strike hard.

The preliminary aerial bombardment of Operation *Cobra* caused heavy losses among the front-line German units, notably the Panzer Lehr; American troops inspect two destroyed armored vehicles—an Sd.Kfz. 251 half-track and a Panther from the 130th Panzer Lehr Regiment. Note the two American dispatch riders napping on their motorbikes. (National Archives)

# In Profile:
# British Tanks

This Churchill Petard tank is armed with a 290mm mortar capable of firing an 18kg projectile, the "flying dustbin," over 230 meters, but devastating at 80 meters or less. This vehicle was used by the Royal Engineers, 79th Armoured Division for close-quarters combat.

Right: A Cromwell belonging to the 2nd Armoured Reconnaissance Battalion, Welsh Guards. This unit was the reconnaissance arm of the Royal Armoured Corps (note the white 45 on a blue and green square), a regiment in the Guards Armoured Division (a white eye on a blue shield). This tank is one of the B Squadron tanks (white is used for the squadron identification square) that landed at the end of June 1944.

A Churchill Mark VII from one of the independent armored brigades charged with supporting the British infantry divisions in their advance.

# Operation *Goodwood*: Montgomery's Tanks to the Fore

There has been much discussion since 1944 on whether Montgomery wanted to achieve a decisive breakthrough with Operation *Goodwood*, or whether he wanted, above all, to deliver a maximum effort east of the bridgehead, days before Operation *Cobra* was unleashed by the Americans. Rather than speculating, it is perhaps beneficial here to consider the battle orders for *Goodwood*, as outlined by Montgomery and his general staff

    i.    aerial bombing from 6.30 a.m. to 8.15 a.m. by heavy and medium bombers

    ii.    51st (Highland) Division to take Colombelles

    iii.    2nd (Canadian) Division to cross the Orne to establish a bridgehead at Vaucelles and at Giberville

    iv.    3rd (British) Division to capture Touffréville, Sannerville, Banneville and Emjéville by descending due south by way of Escoville and attacking from the east to protect thc lcft flank of thc VIII Corps

    v.    VIII Corps to dominate and destroy all armored enemy forces in the region of Bourguébus, Vimont, and Bretteville-sur-Laize, and to be ready to exploit to the south

    vi.    29th Armoured Brigade to advance to the Cagny sector, bypassing east of Cuverville and Demouville that are to be captured by 159th Brigade. Leaving behind an armored regiment, the 11th Armoured Division to establish itself in the perimeter to include Bras, Rocquancourt, and the Beauvoir Farm, but excluding Fontenay-le-Marmion

    vii.    Guards Armoured Division to advance behind the 29th Armoured Brigade in the Cagny sector, then to capture Vimont in the van

A Panzer IV of the 2nd SS Panzer Division abandoned at the side of a road during Operation *Cobra*. It is being examined by GIs next to a 2nd Armored Division Jeep. (National Archives)

viii. 7th Armoured Division to advance behind the Guards Armoured Division via Cagny and Soliers, to control the Hogue, a wooded area northeast of Secqueville, Saint-Aignan de Cramesnil, Garcelles, and Secqueville.

# *Goodwood* and *Cobra* in Parallel

These plans call for comment. First of all, it was the most powerful attack to be delivered by the Allied armored divisions since the landings. Although *Epsom* had constituted almost as large a force—an autonomous armored brigade contained almost as many tanks as an armored division—two of the *Goodwood* armored brigades were to be held in reserve: their use was not foreseen in the initial phases of the operation; and, moreover, the three infantry divisions only had a supplementary role: to hold the flanks of the axis of the offensive.

Everything rested on the 11th, Guards and 7th Armoured Divisions. Of the three, the Guards were the least experienced, and had not yet been battle-tested, having only begun their landings on June 30. The 11th Armoured Division had the most difficult task, leading the assault on Bourguébus.

It was clear that Montgomery's main aim was to destroy the German armor in the Caen sector, the exploitation of the breakthrough to the south being only given five words in the plan. Once again, it was a case of drawing as many German armored divisions as possible to face the British while General Omar Bradley prepared for Operation *Cobra*.

A half-track rolls through the streets of Coutances. The Sherman on the verge has had its white star painted over in green to make it less visible. (National Archives)

(PhotosNormandie)

# In Profile:
# Lieutenant-General Henry Crerar

General Henry Duncan Graham Crerar CH, CB, DSO, CD, PC, or "Harry," was born in 1888 in Hamilton, Ontario. With an engineering background, he then switched career and entered the military, graduating from the Royal Military College, in Kingston, Ontario. He saw action on the Western Front during World War I as a lieutenant-colonel of artillery. Between the wars, he attended the Staff College, Camberley and the Imperial Defence College. He became Director of Military Operations and Military Intelligence in 1935. On the outbreak of war, he was commandant of his alma mater, the Royal Military College.

He served on the Canadian General Staff in England and, by the close of 1940, was Chief of the General Staff. Promoted major-general, he became GOC 2nd Canadian Infantry Division in 1941 before taking command, as a lieutenant-general, of I Canadian Corps the following year in the Italian campaign. In March 1944, he assumed command of the Canadian First Army in England that included, among others, the British I Corps and the Polish 1st Armoured Division. Held in reserve by Montgomery in the early days of the Normandy campaign, First Army then saw action at the Falaise Pocket, the Battle of the Scheldt, the Battle of the Reichswald Forest, the liberation of the Netherlands and ultimately the invasion of Germany. Crerar died in Ottawa in 1965.

(John Downey, U.S.
Office of War Information
/ RMN-Grand Palais
(Château de Blérancourt)
/ Gérard Blot)

# In Profile:
# Major General Philippe Leclerc

Philippe François Marie Leclerc de Hauteclocque, or, more commonly, Leclerc or le maréchal Leclerc, was born to aristocracy in 1902 in Belloy-Saint-Léonard, France. He graduated from the Saint-Cyr military academy in 1924 and saw service in the French-occupied Ruhr, and in Morocco where he was awarded the Croix de Guerre for actions against rebels in the Bou Amdoun mountain region. In 1940 he fought in the Battle for France before escaping to England where he became one of de Gaulle's principal Free French officers. It was here that he adopted the *nom de guerre* Leclerc to protect his family in France against Nazi reprisals.

Sent to French Equatorial Africa, he rallied local leaders against the Vichy French in Gabon before moving to Chad where he conducted operations against the Italian occupation of Libya, with the battle of Kufra being a notable success. In North Africa, his unit became known as L Force, supporting the Eighth Army advance into Tunisia. After the battles on the Mareth Line, L Force became the Deuxième Division Blindée, the 2nd Armored Division, but was generally referred to as La Division Leclerc. The division fought with valour in the Normandy campaign and was prominent in the liberation of Paris, also participating in the liberation of Strasbourg.

In May 1945 he assumed command of the French Far East Expeditionary Corps and was the French representative at the Japanese surrender in Tokyo Bay. He then served in French Indochina, recognizing that only a political solution was workable for the burgeoning conflict, before being recalled to France in 1946. Aged 45, he was killed in an air crash in Algeria in 1947.

# In Profile:
# Self-Propelled Artillery

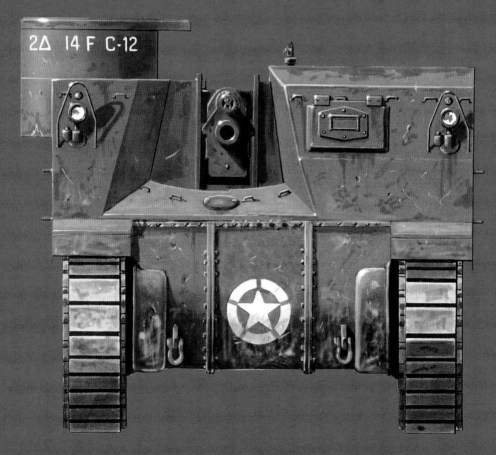

This American M7 Priest, belonged to the 14th Armored Field Battalion, 2nd Armored Division, as indicated by the series of numbers and symbols painted in white at the top of its turret.

A British Sexton (25-pounder gun, self-propelled, tracked) that was allocated to the field artillery regiments (Royal Artillery) of the armored divisions in Normandy. Based on the same chassis as the American M7, several details differentiated the two vehicles. The Sextons were frequently mounted onto Canadian Ram chassis, the driver's post was on the right (not the left), the turret was absent, and the American 105mm gun was replaced with the British 25-pounder.

This American M7 Priest, in profile, may have belonged to the 78th Field Artillery Battalion of the 2nd. It could equally have belonged to the 54th, 67th or 391st Armored Field Artillery Battalion of the 3rd Armored Division that also fought in Operation *Cobra*.

The forces facing VIII Corps were: on the front line, the 272nd Infantry Division, and the 16th Air Landing Division; immediately behind them was the 21st Panzer Division, which had 60 tanks and support of the 503rd Heavy Panzer Battalion and their Tigers; and III Flak Corps and their 88mm guns, used in an antitank capacity: all this constituted a formidable defense. Finally, several kilometers behind the front, the 1st SS Panzer Division (Leibstandarte Adolf Hitler) was held in reserve, ready to intervene.

## An Incomplete Breakthrough

Operation *Goodwood* was, in reality, doomed from day one, despite its scale.

As the news coming through during the first few hours of battle was all good, Montgomery indulged in a certain sense of euphoria, which was conveyed to London by the war correspondents in France, with headlines such as "Second Army Breaks Through," and "Armoured Forces Now in Open Ground, Montgomery Satisfied."

In reality, the armored divisions had barely made it past the front-line lanes of advance, which was not nearly enough given the depth of the German defense. The disappointment that followed the earlier jubilation would provoke a crisis at a much higher level. To explain the failure at Bourguébus, after such a promising start, Montgomery's critics—he had many—placed the blame directly at his door. Many felt it was his lack of fighting spirit that caused the operation to fail, and senior officers hoped that Eisenhower would dismiss him.

The brouhaha at the Supreme Headquarters Allied Expeditionary Force (SHAEF) traveled far enough that the British war cabinet was worried, and sent an HQ representative

A famous photograph of an M7 Priest alongside the elaborate grave of an *unterscharführer*, a corporal or junior squad leader, from the 9th battery of the 17 Artillery Regiment, Götz von Berlichingen Division, killed in the Marchésieux sector on June 17, 1944, probably in an air raid. (National Archives)

An M18 Hellcat tank destroyer, the new "fighter tank" of the American Tank Destroyer Battalion—more maneuverable and just as efficient as the M10—that began its operational career in Normandy. (National Archives)

to visit Montgomery. The general's precarious position ended on July 24 at the Tactical Headquarters in France, when a two-hour meeting between Montgomery and Churchill ended with the former persuading the prime minister not to fire him.

In fact, Montgomery's detractors were wrong to accuse him of lacking fighting spirit. The main reason for the failure of *Goodwood* was its starting position: attacking a salient so far from the main battlefield was completely against the doctrine of warfare. The narrowness of the front caused a monstrous bottleneck that forced the armored divisions to fight as if in a queue; the 7th Armoured Division, for example, barely fired a shot in anger but still managed to lose two tanks on the first day.

As for the failure itself, the details are still up for debate. Certainly, the objectives of July 18 were not all reached and the 29th Brigade suffered serious losses, including 58 percent of its tanks. But as for the rest, the Guards Division lost less than 50 tanks and the 7th Armoured just two Cromwells.

Infantry losses were so minor as to be nearly insignificant: the three battalions of the 159th Infantry Brigade, 11th Armoured Division lost only 16 men.

As for the motorized battalion of the 29th Brigade, the 8th Battalion, Rifle Brigade, noted only four dead, as it had followed the tanks' advance in half-tracks. So, all things considered, it was hardly a disaster. The numbers presented here, based on archival research, are irrefutable; British losses on the first day of *Goodwood* did not exceed 160 tanks, with fewer than 300 casualties across the three armored divisions involved in the battle.

For the Germans, tank losses are generally believed to have been around 50, divided between the 21st Panzer Division, 1st SS Panzer Division, and the 503rd Heavy Panzer Battalion. Infantry losses, however, were comparable to the British: the 16th Air Landing Division had simply ceased to exist. The 272nd Infantry Division fared little better, especially since its survivors, driven toward Caen, were attacked by the Canadians, who had crossed the Orne, and taken Vaucelles and directed themselves southwards.

A Priest from the 4th Armored Division rolls through Coutances. It is the eighth vehicle of B Battery, 66th Armored Field Artillery Battalion, as indicated by the inscription on the turret. In the background, an M5 Stuart has been blown up by a mine. (National Archives)

Finally, British pressure did necessitate the transfer of 9th SS Panzer Division (Hohenstaufen) to the east of the Orne, which was where the Americans were assembling en masse.

# Operation *Cobra*

While Montgomery was being held in check in Operation *Goodwood*, the Americans were preparing to strike a decisive blow.

Bradley's plan, *Cobra*, was of a different breed to that of Montgomery's *Goodwood*. It is true that their ambitions were not the same: Bradley wanted to, and did, break through the front.

The initial phase consisted of a massive aerial bombardment, to open a corridor 2.5 kilometers deep and six wide. Soon after the bombing, two infantry divisions would take control of the front line and consolidate the two flanks of the attack. The armored divisions would then be launched into the breach and the final exploitation would be entrusted to the VII, VIII and XIX Corps.

The scale of *Cobra* was more impressive than that of *Goodwood*, and the initial attack, carried out by the infantry, avoided submitting the tanks to the same dangers as the 11th Armoured. German defenses would be taken by the infantry.

On the German side, the Das Reich had 50 tanks, while the Götz von Berlichingen had no more than 20 self-propelled StuG III assault guns. As for the Panzer Lehr and the 1st Battalion, 6th Panzer Regiment, they had around 80 Panzers, bringing the total to around 150 tanks.

The offensive was to open at 1300 hours on July 24 with the aerial bombardment. In anticipation General Collins, commander of VII Corps, pulled his infantry back by around 1,000 meters to minimize the risk to his troops. But the weather was poor, and the 1,586 bombers were recalled. However, the message failed to reach 352 of the aircraft, and the pilots carried out the attacks anyway. Due to the cloud cover, the raid missed its mark and accidently hit the American lines: 16 men were killed and 60 wounded, though some sources put the figures higher at 25 dead and 131 wounded.

Paradoxically, this untimely bombing did not alarm Bayerlein, head of the Panzer Lehr, in spite of suffering 350 casualties and ten tanks either lost or damaged. In addition, Collins's troops had reoccupied their previous front-line positions to prevent the Germans gaining ground. The entire action gave the impression that a massive offensive was about to be unleashed and that it could be repelled without much trouble on the Germans' part. For Bayerlein, the Americans had showed their hand, and even if they renewed their assault the next day, he felt it could be stopped. He did not imagine that another bombing raid, one of an altogether greater intensity, was on the cards. Nevertheless, his whole division held itself in a state of alertness.

The next day, at 0900 hours, the 1,586 bombers returned to the skies, but this time, they dropped their entire payload. Around 20 aircraft missed their targets, killing 102 American soldiers and wounding three hundred and eighty. But the others found the German lines, with all the effect that one might imagine. However, the victims of the bombing were, in the

July 25, 1944: the first day of Operation *Cobra*. A half-track with American infantry in camouflage fatigues prepares to advance. These men probably belonged to the 41st Armored Infantry Regiment, 2nd Armored Division. (IWM PL 31154)

# In Profile:
# Tanks of the 2nd French Armored Division

"Lion," an M10 tank destroyer of
the 1st Platoon, 2nd Squadron,
Marine Fusiliers Armored
Regiment. This tank was
destroyed on August 12, 1944 in
the Alençon region.

"Grenoble," an M3A3 Stuart from the 1st Squadron, 12th Cuirassiers Regiment, 2nd Armored Division, number 420462.

"Ile de France," an M4A3 Sherman of the 2nd Platoon, 3rd Squadron, 1st African Combat Regiment (Régiment de Chasseurs d'Afrique) of the 2nd French Armored Division, destroyed near Alençon on August 12, 1944—one of the first losses recorded by the 2nd French Armored.

A Sherman in the streets of Avranches, July 31, 1944. Once Bradley realized the extent of his troops' breakthrough, he ordered Patton to redirect the Third Army to the east; Brittany was no longer a principal objective. (IWM EA 31781)

main, independent strongpoints, which limited the devastation somewhat. After the war, Bayerlein wrote that his division had been wiped out by the raid. This was probably an attempt to justify the outcome of the operation; the Panzer Lehr barely lost 2,500 men, and still had 15 of the 40 tanks originally available on the front line.

Even the U.S. 30th Infantry Division, who attacked in the immediate aftermath, admitted that the bombing had not caused a huge number of German casualties, but it had, however, caused considerable chaos, cutting lines of communication and preventing all reinforcement and supply. The infantry found the Germans still well dug in and very much in business.

The terrain, torn apart by the tons of bombs, caused problems for the assailants, who barely advanced over the course of July 25. Here and there, they were stopped by handfuls of German troops clustered around machine guns, in a crater or in the shelter of a hedgerow, or in a ditch.

A study of the topography of the battlefield shows that the terrain was hilly and favored the defenders. This was probably why the Americans did not bypass Montreuil-sur-Lozon and La Chapelle-en-Juger, a diversion of between one and a half and two kilometers. The attackers were being extremely cautious, clearing every piece of ground as they advanced. This was a tactic that would prove profitable, as the next day, the terrain was completely open to exploitation by tanks.

# July 26, 1944

For the American armored force, July 26, 1944 was an important date: launched into the breach, they penetrated deeply into the German front.

The two heavy armored divisions were engaged on the day. The CCB of the 3rd Armored quickly reached Marigny, around six kilometers from the start line, while the CCA of the 2nd Armored captured Saint-Gilles, then Canisy and Saint-Samson de Bonfossé, a village situated approximately ten kilometers south of Saint-Lô.

General von Choltitz, commander of the LXXXIV Corps, had limited reserves with which to counteract the American advance: a regiment of the 353rd Infantry Division and a few elements of the 2nd SS Panzer Division (Das Reich), but his infantry could do nothing in the face of the American deployment.

As for the handful of tanks in the Das Reich, they succumbed at Casigny to the 66th Armored Regiment, supported by aircraft, which, incidentally, once again hit their own troops as well as the enemy. For the time being, however, American losses were light.

On the extreme west of the American front, along the English Channel, the 79th and 8th Infantry Divisions captured Lessay and defeated the 243rd Infantry Division.

This was no longer just a breakthrough in one sector but, thanks to the huge breach that had opened to the south and west of Saint-Lô, a full-scale encirclement. Choltitz was so conscious of this development that he ordered a retreat toward Coutances, and then the establishment of a second line of defense on the Bréhal–Gavray axis, 30 kilometers to the south.

# Toward Encirclement

The offensive continued into July 27. The 2nd Battalion, 66th Armored Regiment was stalled for most of the morning outside Mesnil-Herman, where an antitank barrage proved particularly resilient. Pak guns and, it seemed, several tanks completely halted the Americans' progress, setting fire to three Shermans. Finally, the ground was cleared by noon, and the advance continued with the capture of Mesnil-Opac.

To the west, the CCB of the 2nd Armored Division advanced over ten kilometers during the day, reaching Pont-Brocard on the Soulles.

General Isaac D. White, commander of the CCB, had received the order to charge toward Bréhal to cut off the German retreat. His unit therefore became the de facto vanguard for the entire VII Corps.

This rapid advance met with some resistance, first of all at Quibou, where four Panthers destroyed an M7 Priest and captured several troops, including a sergeant carrying a map of the division's objectives; but with the aid of a group of Thunderbolts, the position was overwhelmed and the Panthers retreated.

Farther away, at Dangy, the Americans rushed through the town, destroying several (empty) general staff cars. They were unaware that Bayerlein himself was in a meeting in one of the houses; he managed to escape as night fell.

General George S. Patton at Coutances, on his way to take command of the Third Army, whereupon he would make the most of the breakthrough at Avranches, plunging unstoppably into the French interior and overseeing the encirclement of German Seventh Army and Fifth Panzer Army. (IWM EA 33213)

Farther west still, the 3rd Armored was also making the most of the breakthrough. The first CCB elements had already arrived at Camprond, less than ten kilometers from Coutances.

To face the looming encirclement, the two elite divisions Das Reich and Götz von Berlichingen, alongside the 243rd and 91st Infantry Divisions., established a north–south line of defense from Montcuit. Thanks to their experience from the Eastern Front, they were experts in re-establishing fractured fronts. This time, the task was beyond even their capabilities, but they did manage to cause heavy matériel losses on the American side.

Thus, in Lorey, SS Sergeant Ernst Barkmann surprised a column of CCB, 3rd Armored, destroying shot by shot three Shermans and various other vehicles. Attacked by Thunderbolts, Barkmann's Panther 424 was hit, but he was able to free it up and destroyed six more Shermans in the streets of Coutances.

On July 28, the threat of encirclement transformed into hard reality for the Germans. In full retreat they were incapable of containing the Americans, whose superior mobility was plain to see.

So it was that the CCA, 2nd Armored Division reached Villebaudon, where it met advance elements of a panzer division that had just arrived at the scene, the 2nd Panzer Division.

The CCB fell on Saint-Denis-le-Gast and Lengronne, ten kilometers from the coast, south of Coutances: the pocket was practically closed. After the capture of Périers and Lessay, Bradley had launched into battle the 6th Armored Division, taking the coastal route, and the 4th Armored, who took the Périers–Coutances road.

At the end of the day, the 4th Armored entered the suburbs of Coutances, while the 6th Armored came to halt four kilometers away.

The Americans had successfully formed a pocket, the rough perimeter of which stretched from the sea to Coutances, then followed the course of the Soulles river to Cerisy,

"Fury" belonged to the 4th Armored Division. It found itself with little to do after the success of Operation *Cobra* and symbolized the new phase of the battle of Normandy, that of a war of movement. (National Archives)

where it veered south, as far as Saint-Denis-le-Gast, via Roncey. It was this little village that gave its name to the renowned "pocket" in the battle for Normandy.

# The Roncey Pocket

Within the fluctuating perimeter of this pocket was a pell-mell of elements from the 2nd SS Panzer Division Das Reich, the 17th SS Panzergrenadier Division Götz von Berlichingen, and the 91st and 243rd Infantry Divisions, as well as paratroopers from the II Parachute, or Meindl, Corps. For all of these units, there was only one chance of salvation: break through the American line to the south.

Facing the trapped Germans was the 2nd Armored Division, which held the line from Saint-Denis-le-Gast to the Siena river. This was the only way out for the Germans, and the Americans were well aware of it. From the evening of July 28, arrangements were made for a stand against the looming—and now desperate—attack by the Waffen SS, notably the Das Reich division; nearly all of its infantry was trapped in the pocket.

The first assault took place on July 29 at around 0400 hours, when a German self-propelled gun attempted to clear a path through the Saint-Martin-de-Cenilly sector. It took sequentially the various positions and strongpoints of the 41st American Armored Infantry Regiment; at the same time the German infantry delivered a frontal attack that deeply penetrated the 41st Regiment, before it was finally stopped. The self-propelled gun—a Marder, most likely—was neutralized by tank fire, and the German infantry retreated at dawn, leaving behind 17 dead and 150 wounded.

The second assault began at 0900 hours, several kilometers away at Pinetière, a small road junction. Around 15 panzers, accompanied by several hundred paratroopers and SS stormtroopers, attacked a company of the 4th Infantry Division and clashed with the 78th Armored Infantry Battalion, supported by four M10s and an antiaircraft section. The fighting was bitter. Antiaircraft M16s fired quadruple 12.7mm guns into the German infantry, and all the artillery pieces were lowered to flat trajectory. For 30 minutes, the battle raged on indecisively. Finally, the intervention of the 41st Infantry Regiment saved the American position.

The Germans were forced back into the interior of the pocket, having lost 126 men and nine tanks. Losses in the 4th Infantry and 2nd Armored Divisions were probably on a comparable scale. While the attempts to break through en masse had failed, several groups of German soldiers escaped into the *bocage*, terrain that lent itself particularly well to this type of warfare: in daylight hours, with the Allied tactical aviation dominating the battlefield, movement was out of the question and the Germans preferred to dig in and wait.

At nightfall the Germans made their move. Thus, a little before midnight on July 29, a group of panzergrenadiers from the Das Reich and Götz von Berlichingen divisions, supported by armored vehicles, rushed the 2nd Battalion, 41st Armored Infantry Regiment. The breakthrough was so deep that the unit's command post was overrun, and Lieutenant Colonel Wilson D. Coleman was killed (after he had destroyed a German panzer with a bazooka).

The Germans then clashed with elements of the 3rd Battalion, 67th Armored Regiment. Caught by surprise, the Americans were quickly forced to retreat, losing in the process several vehicles that were set ablaze by panzerfausts and canon fire.

Finally, the German advance was halted by a mixed force, comprising divisional reserves and survivors of the two units defeated by the Germans earlier that night.

The Germans were now attempting desperate sorties and it was during the night of July 29/30 that the 2nd Armored Division reported their heaviest losses of Operation *Cobra*. Yet, come daybreak, the line was still intact; it had been held at no mean cost, and the surrounded troops, who were now in desperate need of food and munitions, began to surrender.

During the five days of Operation *Cobra*, Combat Command B of the 2nd Armored Division had neutralized 1,500 German troops, captured a further 5,200, and destroyed 331 vehicles. Its own losses were 42 killed, 69 missing and 284 wounded.

While the 2nd Armored Division was tasked with clearing the Roncey Pocket, the three other American armored divisions began moving south. The 3rd Armored launched its CCB to the southeast: by the end of the day, was in sight.

The 6th Armored Division travelled along the coast; having taken Bréhal it was now on the approach to Grainville. But it was the 4th Armored Division that achieved the most that day: hurtling down from Coutances, it liberated Cérences, then Haye-Pesnel, and entered Avranches by evening, more than 40 kilometers in a day.

The German front had been definitively broken: the Americans encountered little in the way of further opposition, while they landed more and more armored divisions: on August 1, the 2nd French Armored Division was ready for combat, followed on August 2 by the 5th Armored Division and several days later by the 7th Armored.

In all, seven armored divisions, mostly intact, were launched into the breach. The battle of Normandy was drawing to a close and war of movement beginning.

# | Afterword

Almost a month after D-Day, by 4 July 1944, the Allies had landed over a million troops in Normandy. Yet it would be a further six weeks before the Germans were driven out of the province, from their last-ditch laager in the Falaise Gap. Why, with the vast industrial resources of the Allies, overwhelming air power, and unlimited reserves of manpower, did it take so long? A microcosm of the Normandy campaign was Caen, a city that was supposed to have been taken by the evening of D-Day, on June 6, yet several weeks later was still in German hands.

Although the Allied troops were, in the main, untested in battle, there can be no questioning their resolve. That they were up against hardened Waffen SS stormtroopers and that ultimately they were victorious, is a measure of their fighting spirit—tankers and infantry in equal measure. Not only did they have to endure the challenges of the *bocage* hedgerows, unsuited for mobile armored warfare, but they also had to face the ravages of their own inexperienced air forces, suffering "friendly fire" casualties that numbered in the thousands.

That General Omar Bradley's Americans triumphed, magnificently so, in Operation *Cobra*, which itself led to the closure of the Falaise Pocket that ultimately heralded a comprehensive German defeat, cannot be attributed to Bernard Montgomery's generalship. As overall commander of the land forces, he must take responsibility for the earlier failures of operations *Epsom* and *Goodwood*. It was only through the grace and good offices of his prime minister that he was spared the ignominy of dismissal, perversely receiving a promotion to field marshal—over the head of his immediate superior, General Eisenhower—later in September (and thus being permitted to embark upon the disastrous Operation *Market Garden* and directly causing the Dutch famine of 1944/5 that killed some 22,000 civilians by failing to neutralize the German forces of occupation in The Scheldt).

It was the stated Allied desire, and goal, that the war would be over by the close of 1944. It could have been, certainly on the Western Front, and perhaps therefore, by extension, on the Eastern Front too. But the ripple effects of Caen—the failures of *Epsom* and *Goodwood*—would ensure that the war would drag on well into the spring of 1945, some 11 months after D-Day.

# | Further Reading

Beevor, Anthony. *D-Day: The Battle for Normandy*. New York: Viking, 2009

Guderian, Heinz. *Panzer Leader*. New York: E. P. Dutton & Co., 1952

Hastings, Max. *Overlord: D-Day and the Battle for Normandy*. New York: Simon & Schuster, 1984.

https://legionmagazine.com/en/2009/05/

https://ww2db.com

Keegan, John. *Six Armies in Normandy: From D-Day to the Liberation of Paris, June 6th–August 25th, 1944*. London: Pimlico, 2004

Mattson, Gregory L. *SS-Das Reich: The History of the Second SS Division 1941–45*. London: Amber Books, 2002

Mellenthin, F. W. von. *Panzer Battles: A Study of Employment of Armor in the Second World War*. Oklahoma: University of Oklahoma Press, 1956

# | Index

# WITHDRAWN